TOURISM

Investment Growth and Careers

TOURISM
Investment Growth and Careers

B.S. Badan
Harish Bhatt

Commonwealth

Tourism : Investment Growth and Careers

Edition : 2026

ISBN 81-311-0064-2

Published by :

COMMONWEALTH PUBLISHERS
4831/24, Prahlad Street,
Ansari Road, Darya Ganj,
New Delhi - 110002
Ph. : 23275511, 23257835
e-mail : commonwealthbooks@gmail.com

Typesetting by :
Rishu Computers
Delhi

Printed at :
Roshan Offset Printers
Delhi

Preface

Tourism can be defined as the act of travel for the purpose of recreation, and the provision of services for this act. It is a service industry, comprising a number of tangible and intangible components. The tangible elements include transportation systems—air, rail, road, water and now, space; hospitality services, accommodation, foods and beverages, tours, souvenirs; and related services such as banking, insurance and safety and security. The intangible elements include: rest and relaxation, culture, escape, adventure, new and different experiences.

Travel and tourism is a major industry in the world and is at the top of the league of invisible earners of foreign currency. Many sovereignties, along with their respective countries and states, depend heavily upon travel expenditures by foreigners as a source of taxation and income for the enterprises that sell services to these travellers. Consequently the development of tourism is often a strategy employed either by a non-governmental organization or a governmental agency to promote a particular region for the purpose of increasing commerce through exporting goods and services to non-locals.

During recent years the tourism industry has witnessed unprecedented growth. Increasing consumer demand for educational and participatory travel experiences has resulted in a variety of specialty niche markets such as ecotourism, cultural-heritage tourism, and agritourism. New paradigms link strategic tourism planning with sustainable development.

The leisure and tourism industry is one of the leading global economic activities, a multi-billion-dollar industry with

700 million international travellers per year around the world. Tourism is a motor for employment and income creation and, especially in poor countries, a vehicle for development. But today it is not sufficient to simply create employment without regard for the quality of jobs and the social and environmental effects of tourism in vulnerable areas. A growing number of organizations, including the tourism industry leadership, are increasingly conscious of the risks and are adopting a more responsible attitude.

The present publication provides an authoritative look at how to manage travel and tourism industry in a better way. It introduces the complexities of the tourism system so that they will be better positioned to eventually assume the managerial challenges and responsibilities in a diverse and challenging industry. The latest advancements in tourism theory and thinking, retaining the thoroughness of content, diversity of applications, regional and international issues, economic significance, tourism operators and the role of technology in the tourism industry etc. are also described elaborately. Numerous regional and global case studies and examples are included to provide an appropriately broad geographic context. This work will be highly informative and useful to students, researchers, policy makers, managers and working groups of travel and tourism industry.

B.S. Badan
Harish Bhatt

CONTENTS

CONTENTS

1

THE TRAVEL AND TOURISM INDUSTRY

There originally was some confusion in the common uses of the words *travel, transportation* and *tourism.* This confusion was aggravated in the period of America's early affluence, when some tourists who had acquired riches before they acquired culture made themselves ridiculous by their uncouth manners, loud voices, and conspicuous consumption, particularly when they were travelling in Europe. As a result, many tourists preferred to be called travellers, and tourist agencies became travel agencies, tourist bureaus became visitors' bureaus, and so forth.

Today, this artificial distinction has largely eroded away, and these words can now be used with their real meanings. A tourist no longer feels insulted to be called a tourist, and numerous governmental offices call themselves tourist promotion bureaus.

Further interesting definitions of these words are used at Niagara University's College of Hospitality and Tourism Management. *Transportation* is defined as the movement of goods; *travel* is defined as the movement of people; and *tourism* concerns the entire business of leisure travel and related supporting activities.

This book concentrates on careers in all three of these broad fields, but selects those in which the work requires travel, direct service to travellers or vacationers, or promotion of travel and destinations. Thus, we shall discuss careers in the merchant marine because they entail travel, even though 97 per cent of the workers on U.S. oceangoing ships are on tankers and freighters, and only 3 per cent are on passenger ships. We shall omit consideration of workers in fields such as aircraft and automobile manufacture and auto repair. They serve the travelling public, but not directly, and little or no travel is required for their work.

Origin and Development of Travel

Travel has always been an important feature of people's lives. Historically, what we would call business travel began, in the most primitive sense, with staying alive—travel to obtain food. As civilisation advanced, travel became a means to promote trade, consolidate governments and provide communication.

Great migrations of peoples took place after disasters such as lava flows or floods had devastated their lands. This was business travel of the purest sort—they had to find new lands that would support them. Nomads in semiarid lands seldom stayed long in one place because their grazing animals would soon consume all the vegetation. Many groups of people who herded animals, such as the Laplanders with their reindeer, moved twice every year between summer pastures and winter havens.

As people began to specialise in what they could grow or make or mine from the earth, trade developed. The first travelling salespeople were emissaries to find markets for goods and to arrange for caravans or ships to deliver these goods.

Military travel also developed early, as warlike tribes conquered peaceful ones and moved into their territories. As empires grew, soldiers travelled ceaselessly between the capital and the farthest borders to supervise and carry orders and to impose the ruler's will. Regular massenger systems became fast and reliable as early as ancient times in Egypt, developing over the millennia into stagecoach and packet boat networks, the Pony Express, and modern courier and postal systems.

Thus, the stream of travellers has grown constantly—sailors, oxcart drivers, messengers, salespeople, armies, covered-wagon trains, herdskeepers—all intent on carrying on their own work or someone else's.

Another kind of travel developed in medieval times—educational travel. A young person learning a craft was apprenticed to a master craftsperson near home for a period of years to learn the basics; then the apprentice spent a year travelling to the workshops of masters of the craft in other countries, working there for a time to gain more skill and knowledge. Upon returning from these travels, the apprentice became a journeyman—one who had travelled and learned. Similarly, the typical university student would spend a "wander-year" visiting universities in other countries, studying under the most illustrious professors to be found, and polishing skills in one or two foreign languages. Travel thus achieved a new dimension, being performed not only for essential purposes, but to improve skill and knowledge.

Other non-business travel was done for health reasons. Ancient Romans travelled to spas in Italy, Austria and France seeking remedies for their ailments in curative water or mud. Only the wealthy could do this, of course, but physicians for hundreds of years have been prescribing travel as one way of improving health. They found that a change of air, of climate, of associations made people feel stronger. Europe's spas, which fell out of favour with American doctors as medial practice grew more scientific in the twentieth century, are not only still in business, but are attracting more people than ever before, including the patients of American doctors.

Travel for the pure pleasure of it—tourism—has been one of the special privileges of the rich since ancient times. Europe's spas, in addition to being health centers, were also social centers, with balls, picnics, plays and concerts. They become more and more popular after stagecoaches were replaced by comfortable trains and sailing vessels by reliable steamships.

In America, too, there was summer travel by the rich to spas in Virgina, Pennsylvania and Arkansas, as well as to summer estates at the seashore or in the mountains. The grand tour of Europe, which had become a tradition for aristocratic British students upon their graduation from Oxford or Cambridge, became a fashionable once-in-a-lifetime excursion of six months to a year for America's new industrial, mining and railroad millionaires.

Wars have also stimulated travel. The Crusades, for example, gave Europe an interest in the Middle East that lasted for centuries, with trade and business travel flourishing between military campaigns. It was World War I that really brought intercontinental travel down to prices that middle-class Americans could afford, travel having piqued the interest of the millions of Americans who went to Europe to fight. Steamships were in their heyday, and the war had built up their passenger-carrying capacities.

At the same time, wide-ranging domestic travel came within the reach of Americans with the proliferation of inexpensive automobiles aned hard-surfaced roads. As the automobile enabled people to travel further afield, such expensive resorts as Lakewood and Cape May, New Jersey, to which the wealthy had travelled by train from nearby cities, suddenly lost trade. Florida and southern California became destinations for mass travel, and many people began to travel during the winter to good mountain slopes for skiing. As a result, there was a burgeoning of beach, mountain and ski resorts.

Then came World War II. Many millions of young American men and women were sent to Britain and all over Europe, to Hawaii, Alaska, the Philippines, China, India, Australia and New Zealand, the islands of the Pacific, North Africa and the Middle East, and finally, to conquered Japan, Germany and Italy. These young people were fascinated with what they saw and did in other lands, and, naturally, they wanted to go back.

During the war years, aviation had come into its own. After the war aerial troop transports were converted to serve the new travelling public as passenger aircraft, giving Americans a new kind of opportunity—travel to Europe for a vacation of only two weeks. U.S. aircraft factories converted to the manufacture of passenger planes and soon were supplying them to the new airlines that were springing up all over the world.

Travel now was possible for just about any Americans who wanted it—in their won cars throughout most of North America or on low-priced excursion and charter flights to other continents. Worldwide tourism increased 1,000 per cent from 1950 to 1970, a phenomenal advance. To support this increase, there had to be a commensurate increase in the infrastructure that sustains tourism and attracts tourists—hotels, gambling casinos, amusement parks, marinas, airports, highways, beach facilities, ski resorts, aircraft, buses, cars, restaurants, entertainment and sports facilities, rental cars and boats, and a host of less visible items such as electricity, gas, telephone and water supply systems in resort areas.

War-torn Germany and Japan, starting from rock bottom in 1946, worked hard and rebuilt their economies into powerful positions within twenty years. Profits filtered down, and soon Getman and Japanese tourists were being seen all over the world, alongwith British, French and Italian tourists.

Tourism

Tourism requires some affluence, alongwith the feeling that travel is a desirable and rewarding activity. There are still about three billion people in the world who have neither the incentive nor the means to travel because their lives are totally occupied with the struggle for survival. And in many countries, citizens may have the intellectual curiosity and perhaps even the means to travel, but it is forbidden, except on the business of the government or on government-sponsored projects. Citizens of the United States tend to take travel for granted, but we should bear in mind that to the world's economically depressed and politically suppressed majority, it is an unattainable luxury.

Travel is coming to be regarded as a necessity in North America. Inflation in Europe and America, Severe dollar devaluation, and an oil shortage imposed by the Arab nations reduced the number of Americans travelling to Europe in 1974 by 10 to 15 per cent from the level of just a few years before. But Americans did not stop travelling. During the severest part of the oil shortage, people went to resorts near home, and many of these recreational areas had record years. The oil shortage eased, but unemployment and inflation worsened during the winter of 1974-75; yet Florida and other southern areas were jammed with tourists.

Dr. Louis F. Twardzik, Chairman of the Department of Park and Recreation Resources at Michigan State University, said: "The great number of tourists crowding Florida resorts this winter wasn't really an unnatural phenomenon in times of social stress. Instead, it is merely and expression of the high value people place on their recreation today. The economic picture is severe enough to trigger a higher demand for recreation by people at all economic levels."

In the oil shortage of 1979, the earlier pattern was repeated. Travel in personal autos was considerably reduced, but this brought bonanza tourist business to resorts close to the cities. For longer journeys, travellers again crowded into buses, ships, trains and aircraft.

Two points are of importance to the person considering a career in travel. First, recreational travel—available only to the rich during most of the world's history—has come to be regarded as a necessity in the United States and Canada for people of the lower middle class as well as for those of the middle and upper classes. It is very broadly based. Second, if travel by certain modes or to certain destinations becomes too expensive or otherwise difficult, people will switch to other modes or destinations, but they will continue to travel for pleasure. This indicates stability for the industry as a whole, regardless of the ups and downs for particular segments.

From 1985 on, it was noticed that people were taking more vacations, albeit shorter ones. Analysts deduced that this resulted from several changes in American life. In many families both husband and wife were working, which made it somewhat more difficult to get away for the traditional two weeks. There were more childless families, which made it easier to take spontaneous long-weekend vacations. There was less total leisure time because many people were working at two jobs, so they had to squeeze in brief vacations as their jobs permitted. The total effect on the tourism business was good because it helped to even out the number of people on vacation at any one time, thus contributing more stability to the business and steadier work for its employees. From 1985 to 1987, weekend trips increased by 46 per cent.

Growth in the Travel and Tourism Industry

Tourism continues to be a major industry of the United States and of many countries of the world. Preliminary 2001 figures by the Travel Industry Association of America (TIA) reported the following statistics:

- The value of the U. S. travel industry is $545 billion.
- Tourism is one of the United States' largest service exports: the $90 billion spent in the United States by international visitors and $82.3 billion spent outside the United States by domestic travellers creates $7.7 billion in American trade surplus.
- Tourism is one of the country's largest employers, with eighteen million Americans directly involved in travel or travel-related jobs.
- Tourism is the first-, second-, or third-largest employer in twenty-nine states.
- Domestic U.S. travel has increased 6 per cent from 1994 to 2000.

The Canadian Tourism Commission (CTC) reported that in 2000 tourism, from both domestic and international sources, has become a significant contributor to the Canadian economy:

- Total tourism revenues equal $54.1 billion.
- Tourism, as a percentage of the GDP, is 2.4 per cent.
- Total direct tourism employment is 546,400, and the growth rate relative to the total business section is 0.5 percentage points faster.

An important demographic trend in the United States that will affect the travel industry in coming decades is the aging of the U.S. population. In 2001 the first of the "baby boom" generation (seventy-eight million people) turned fifty-five years old. This "mature traveller," according to a study conducted in 2000 by the Travel Industry Association entitled "The Mature Traveller (55+)," accounts for nearly one-third of all domestic travel in the United States. Travellers fifty-five years and older took nearly 179 million trips in 1999, up 5 per cent over 1994.

In addition, the U.S. population continues to grow rapidly; from 275 million today it is forecasted to reach 400 million by 2050. Close to 30 per cent of the population is currently under the age of twenty, offering enormous potential for further travel trade. Other trends, such as an increase in double-income households, rising education levels, and an increasing priority in the mindset of many to take vacations to escape the burdens of everyday life, affect a positive growth in travel.

Beyond the fact that travel is a huge and strong industry that should afford a good degree of stability in travel-related work, it has great intangible attraction. People in travel jobs are helping other people to go somewhere special, where they will relax and enjoy themselves. In our sedentary society, there are many who travel to find a challenge for their bodies—skiing, surfing, scuba diving, or mountain climbing.

With equal zest, others travel to find the challenges to the mind that appear in contrasting one's own feelings and actions with those of people in another country. Most groups believe they are inherently superior to others. Travellers make the discovery that theirs is not the only way of life, that they can learn from other cultures, and that their habits and thoughts are not even acceptable to many people. They also find that they can contribute an occasional workable idea in a foreign setting.

The travel worker, whose hours are passed with travellers seeking physical and mental challenge, relaxation, and change, finds constant stimulation form working with travellers and helping them fulfil their desires. Helping others travel stimulates one's own urge to go places, and being in the industry gives one special advantages for personal travel.

Perks in the Travel Industry

A special inducement offered by careers in travel is the possibility of travelling oneself—at nominal cost or totally free, or, better still, being paid to travel. Constant travel with a salary can be enjoyed as a member of a flight crew or a ship's company. Paid seasonal travel is available to tour directors—usually men and women who have worked their way up in a travel agency. Long-haul bus drivers, hostesses, and railroad train crews also are paid for constant travel.

Employees of airlines, passenger shipping lines, passenger rail lines, and bus lines, whether they travel in their jobs or not, usually are given liberal free or reduced-rate personal travel for themselves and their immediate families, beginning soon after they start working.

Travel agency personnel are so important in bringing business to air, rail, ship, and bus companies that these carriers offer them trips at very low rates and may offer free trips to familiarise them with new routes or cruises. Operators of tourist resorts or attractions and national tourism offices of foreign countries also give free familiarisation ("FAM") trips to travel agents and sometimes to their staffs. Very low hotel rates usually are available to travel agency personnel. Additionally, employees of hotel chains usually can stay at their company's hotels at a fraction of the regular rates.

The Broad Variety of Travel Jobs

Transportation, travel and tourism provide work for about one person in seven in the United States. The variety of occupations within the field or those closely allied to it is almost without limit. For example, a doctor, a manicurist, a chef, and a horn player all become part of the travel business if they work on a ship or at a resort such as Disney World.

The travel world, therefore, is not a single profession or vocation, but dozens of professions and occupations. Because travel and tourism is a conglomeration of several service industries, there is no single figure representing the travel and tourism economic output is the U.S. System of National Accounts (the accounting system that reports the gross national product). Two studies were put together in 1997—one for 1992 and the other for 1997—by a newly formed programme called "Travel and Tourism Satellite Account" (TTSA) under the U.S. Department of Commerce. Efforts are currently underway to fund the continuation of these important studies, which also indicate the broad variety of jobs related to travel and tourism, including the following:

Hotels and lodging places
Eating and drinking places
Railroads and related services
Local and suburban transit
Interurban highway passenger transportation
Taxicabs
Racing, including track opration
Marinas
Libraries, museums and art galleries
Botanical and zoological gardens

Air transportation
Water transportation
Automotive rental
Arrangement of passenger transportation
Miscellaneous amusement and recreation services
Motion picture theaters
Dance studios
Schools and halls
Theatrical poducers
Members sports and recreation clubs
Bands, orchestras, and entertainers
Professional sports clubs and promoters
Gasoline service stations
Retail

Education for travel-related work is thus of many different kinds, and there is no single way to prepare for all travel jobs.

As with all large business organisations, marketing is vital to all of the major airlines, cruise lines, bus lines, hotel chains and travel agencies. At the New School for Social Research in New York, the first master's degree programme in Tourism and Travel Administration stresses marketing. The students, midcareer people working in travel, flock to the marketing courses. Marketing includes selling, but goes beyond salesmanship to find out what consumers want, why they prefer one product or hotel or airline over another and much more. The effects on sales of public relations, advertising, merchandising, pricing, economics, airline scheduling, government regulation, and many other factors must be considered by a marketing director. Talented marketing people are directly in line to become vice presidents and presidents of their firms.

In the pages that follow, for each travel industry discussed, you will find information on its main career opportunities, what educational preparation you will need, and the specific steps you should take to get started on your career.

The figures represented in this book come from a variety of sources: the 1997 TTSA report, the U.S. Department of Labour (Bureau of Labour Statistics), and a number of trade associations, state agencies and independent studies.

2

ROLE OF AIRLINES IN TOURISM

The scheduled airlines of the United States form a gargantuan industry, transporting more than 622 million passengers and more than 22 million ton-miles of cargo every year. This is accomplished with the investment of more than $89 billion in aircraft and ground facilities and the dedicated service of more than 670,00 employees.

The events of 11th September, 2001, presented the United States airline industry with unprecedented challenges. Losses to the airline industry have been estimated at more than $7.7 billion in 2001, even with federal government assistance. However, signs of recovery are expected, and the airline industry, used to temporarily weathering losses due to skyrocketing fuel costs, economic recessions, or other factors, will pick up since as expanding population alone is bound to necessitate increasing air traffic.

Airline work is exciting, and the industry is still growing. Pay is fairly high in airline jobs, on average 53 per cent higher than the national average, and working conditions are usually good. The field tends to attract adventurous people, so you are likely to discover social rewards in working with other lively and interesting employees.

Flight Attendants

This position used to be referred to as *stewardess, hostess,* or *steward.* In the past, the employee who served food and drink and attended to passengers' wants on U.S. and Canadian airlines had to be female, unmarried, young, attractive, and (in the early days of aviation) short—because of the low ceilings in passenger craft. At first, airline companies also required that flight attendants be nurses. Today approximately 15 per cent of flight attendants are male, and there is a minimum height requirement on many airlines due to the height of the overhead bins.

According to the Association of Flight Attendants, AFL-CIO, which represents over 50 per cent of the flight attendants of twenty-six airlines, in mid-2002 there were approximately one hundred thousand flight attendants.

Job Responsibilities

A flight attendant's main responsibility is passenger safety—to inform passengers of safety procedures and regulations and to enforce them. A flight attendant's job starts before the flight takes off with a briefing by the pilot on topics such as flight emergency evacuation procedures, weather conditions, or special passenger needs. A thorough check of emergency equipment, food, and beverage supplies and proper cabin conditions follows before the greeting of passengers aboard the plane.

Flight attendants also check passenger lists before takeoff and take care of flight reports, caterers' invoices, and requests for supplies or for special attention to equipment. Before take off, the flight attendant checks that passengers are properly seated and luggage is stored, and announces safety procedures in case of an emergency, such as oxygen and flotation equipment and the location of escape doors. After the flight takes off, the flight attendant serves the meals and drinks; answers questions about the flight; and distributed blankets, reading material, pillows, and so forth, as requested. Special care is given to unaccompanied children, the elderly, and handicapped persons. Prior to landing, an inventory is taken of headsets, alcoholic beverages, and moneys collected; landing announcements are made; and cabin safety checks are ensured for a safe and smooth landing. After the flight, a flight attendant reports on minor medication given to passengers, lost and found articles, and any other subjects that may need to be reported or addressed.

A flight attendant's job is not all glamorous. When a passenger becomes drunk and disorderly or sick, or even goes crazy or dies, it is the flight attendants who must cope with the problems. When there's an emergency landing, flight attendants must deploy slides and evacuate passengers swiftly. And the flight attendant is usually the first person to deal with a hijacker. flight attendants must soothe angry, frightened, or sick passengers; serve drinks and meals as rapidly as possible; and take care of any special needs of passengers or the flight-deck crew. They often must work under tension, and on long trips, they may finish service dinner at midnight and start serving breakfast two hours later. Vacation travel frequently starts Friday evening or Saturday morning and ends Sunday evening, so flight attendants often find themselves working in the sky on weekends instead of having time off.

On the other hand, flight attendants have considerable variety in their work and the added bonus of free or very inexpensive travel. In addition, they generally receive all the fringe benefits available in comparable office jobs.

Requirements

How times have changed! As mentioned above, it was once required that a woman be unmarried to be a flight attendant. Today, on average, a flight attendant must be at least eighteen to twenty-one years of age, married or unmarried. Excellent health, a well-groomed appearance, weight in proportion to height, minimum height to reach overhead bins (which vary by airline/aircraft), and vision corrected to 20/30 or better are the physical requirements of most airlines. Most airlines also give flight crews regular physical examinations, to make sure they remain in good condition and are able to cope with emergencies. Many airlines stress the ability to operate mechanical equipment, aircraft doors and window exits, evaluation slides, life rafts, and fire extinguishers, and they list associated weights for each type of equipment in flight attendant job descriptions. There are some variations in most of these qualifications, so if you don't fit a certain airline's specifications, look for an airline that fits yours.

All airlines stress the importance of professionalism, good customer service, and appearance.

A sample job description from a major U.S. airline states: "A flight attendant is in continuous contact with the public. As a flight attendant, you must perform your duties in a courteous and professional manner. Your are responsible for providing the highest level of customer service to both our internal and external customers. Your behaviour, appearance, and professionalism define our standard of excellence. The culture of our airline is to present a consistent, reliable, professional, customer-driven image."

A sample job description from a Canadian airline states: "The ideal flight attendant candidate presents a well-groomed appearance that is enhanced by a pleasant and outgoing personality. A sincere desire to be of service to customers is essential. The candidate must be pleasant, patient, well-mannered and have had previous experience working with the public. Above all, the flight attendant's role is hightly service-oriented and very vital to the airline's success."

Most airlines required flight attendants to be high school graduates, although some say that a high school diploma or G.E.D. is preferred but not required. In actuality, most airlines want people who have had two years of college, nursing training, or experience in dealing with the public.

In most cases, U.S. immigration policy prevents airlines from considering for employment anyone who is not a U.S. citizen or who is an alien with a permanent visa. Since most airlines have a policy of hiring their own nationals, it is difficult for an American or Canadian to get a job with a European airline, for example, unless he or the has some special required qualification, such as fluency in several languages. Excellent English is expected by all airlines, and if you hope to work on an international route, a fair background in one other language is essential.

Air Canada requires its flight attendants to be Canadian citizens or landed immigrants and be able to speak at least two languages: English, French, and/or one of Air Canada's route languages.

Education and Training

Various private schools offer specialised training for flight attendant jobs, but generally speaking, such programmes are not likely to help get you a job. Every airline either operates its own training facilities or sends its new flight attendants to a school, sometimes operated by another airline with which it has a contract. Training by the airlines is usually four to six weeks. Candidates go through intensive training that covers areas such as government rules and regulations, airline customer service philosophy, in-flight service, aircraft familiarisation, and emergency procedures. Tests are given frequently, and some airlines require that a student must maintain an average of 90 per cent to continue in the training programme.

Once applicants have successfully completed an intensive training programme, they may be assigned to an in-flight service base and are placed on reserve status. Reserve status flight attendants on duty are called in for flight attendants who are sick, on vacation, or have been rerouted. When not on duty, reserves must be available on short notice. Usually a flight attendant is on reserve for one year, but in some cities it can take up to five to ten years to get off reserve and be able to "bid" monthly for regular assignments.

The home base at which a flight attendant lives most of the time is called the *domicile*. This is not a dormitory, but a city in which the employee has an apartment. Oftentimes flight attendants starting out share apartments. If a flight attendant wants to remain permanently in the same city, he or she can choose an airline with short routes—generally called feeder lines—where there's a good chance of getting home to the same bed every night. On the long routes, a flight attendant is likely to spend several nights each month in a hotel room at the far end of the routes.

Earnings, Advancement and Job Outlook

According to the Association of Flight Attendants, in 2002 the median starting pay was $15,174 a year. The Bureau of Labour Statistics states that the median annual earnings of flight attendants were $38,820 in 2000 with the middle 50 per cent earning between $28,200 and $56,610. Pay scales vary by airlines, seniority, and routes. On international flights (where facility in a foreign language is always desired, and often required), pay ranges from 12 to 20 per cent higher. To get current hourly wages based on one's number of years as a flight attendant, refer to the flight attendant union websites (see the Sources of Information section at the end of this chapter).

With most of the major airlines, there is base pay for the first sixty-seven flying hours; and for each further flight hour, up to a maximum of eighty-five hours, there is additional pay. Pay raises are small but regular enough to be counted on and there are allowances for meals away from home, limousines to and from airports and uniform maintenance.

Advancement from the position of flight attendant comes with seniority and merit. The top position in the cabin crew is flight service director. At some airlines there is a special position called *purser,* the person who handles all cash collected during the flight for drinks, earphones and merchandise.

Nonflying positions to which flight attendants can be promoted include jobs as instructor, customer service director and recruiting representative. Flight attendants may be used in photographs by the airline's public relations staff.

Delta, which has historically insisted upon promotion from within, offers one example of promotion possibilities: after three years of flying out of Miami and Atlanta, one stewardess became secretary to Delta's director of engineering. Soon she was promoted to be one of five Delta female sales representatives. Within half a year, she became coordinator of women's services for the airline, overseeing the production of travel information and services to women.

The U.S. Federal Aviation Administration (FAA) views flight attendants not only as people who minister to passengers' creature comforts, but also as guardians of passengers' safety. To ensure passenger protection in case of emergencies, the FAA requires that there be one flight attendant for every fifty seats on an airliner. As aircraft grow in size, the number of flight attendants increases.

In the United States, the Association of Flight Attendants, AFL-CIO, represents the airline attendants of a number of airlines. The Association of Flight Attendants, International Brotherhood of Teamsters (IBT), and the Transport Workers Union of America represent attendants of other airlines. Several airlines have company unions (such as the Association of Professional Flight Attendants for American Airlines or the Association of Flight Attendants—United Airlines). Most flight attendants are union members. In Canada many flight attendants are members of CUPE (Canadian Union of Public Employees) Airlines Division.

In the late 1970s, the unions argued, bargained, and held long strikes. They succeeded in gaining recognition of their professionalism, higher pay, more consideration for their health and maternity problems and improved rest facilities.

After the Airline Deregulation Act took effect at the beginning of 1985, however, the airline business was suddenly much more competitive than before. With no regulation of rates or routes or schedules, airlines were free to engage in rate wars, start new routes, drop service on routes losing money, and cut costs to the bone. One way of cutting costs was to reduce salaries. Continental did this, after much labour strife, by reducing salaries for new hires.

As part of the cost-cutting drive, some airlines started charging a fee for accepting a job application, charging new flight attendants for their uniforms, and charging tuition to attend the flight attendant training school. The airlines also started scheduling flights closer together so that a flight crew would have only a ten-hour layover between flights, instead of a twenty-four-hour respite. Competition among airlines mandated these changes, which led to higher productivity.

According to the Bureau of Labour Statistics, flight attendants jobs are expected to increase by 18.4 per cent between 2000 and 2010. (This estimate was made prior to the events of 11th September, 2001, when many flight attendants were furloughed.)

If travel and flexibility in your schedule are appealing to you, then flight attendant may be a good career choice. However, don't forget that there are drawbacks: within the first three years the pay is not favourable, and you will have little control over your schedule.

Pilots, Copilots and Flight Engineers

According to the FAA, in 2001 there were 265,204 commercial and airline transport pilots and 65,398 flight engineers. Job prospects for major airlines are best for college graduates who have a commercial pilot's licence or flight engineer's licence and experience flying jets.

Job Responsibilities

A job whose glamour is equal to that of the flight attendant is airline pilot. In addition to their prestige, pilots are highly paid, up to $185,000 or more per year. The majority of pilots are captains, first officers (or copilots), and second officers (or flight engineers) who transport passengers and cargo. The rest are commercial pilots with flying responsibilities such as dusting crops, testing aircraft, tracking criminals, or monitoring traffic.

Pilot and Copilot

The commercial airline pilot arrives at the airport well before takeoff time. After getting information from the meteorological office about weather conditions along the flight path, the pilot works out route, speed and altitude in a conference with the airline dispatcher. He or she then coordinates this flight plan with the air traffic controllers. The copilot is generally with the pilot during these conferences and assists as requested in working out practical routes and altitudes.

They proceed to the airplane, where they check the controls, engines, and instruments, going down a long checklist item by item. Passengers board and are strapped in, the cabin-crew chief advises the pilot that they are ready, and the pilot obtains permission from air traffic control to taxi and then to take off. Once airborne, with the assistance of autopilot and the flight management computer, the pilots steer the plane along the planned route. The pilot or copilot makes frequent radio reports to controllers on the ground as to the plane's altitude, speed, and position; the weather; amount of fuel remaining; and anything unusual about the flight. Altitude and speed are changed, as well as the plane's heading, as the pilot deems necessary. Instruments detailing the condition of engines, amount of fuel, altitude, airspeed, and other factors are constantly scrutinised.

In case of an emergency, such as an engine becoming too hot or ice forming on the wings faster than it can be melted, the pilot must take time, distance, fuel and other factors into consideration. Shutting down one engine, for example, will make it take longer to reach the destination. If low fog or clouds obscure the field at the destination, an approach on instruments may be necessary, with a controller on the ground "talking the plane down." Leaving the aircraft after the flight, the pilot and copilot must fill out records of the flight at the airline office before they have completed their day's work.

Some senior pilots become instructors. There is a considerable need for instructors because every time an airline starts using a new model of airplane, pilots must be taught how to fly it. Sometimes the first airline to start using a new model will instruct the pilots of several other airlines.

All categories of licences require recency of experience. The FFA requires that pilots must pass a flight review with an instructor at least every two years. Pilots are often subject to unannounced spot checks by the FAA, and they must take regular six-month FFA/Transport Canada and company flight checks.

Not all pilots in the travel trade fly large passenger planes. Some of them are bush pilots who still "fly by the seat of their pants" to wilderness lakes, perhaps carrying a couple of fishermen whose canoe is lashed to the undercarriage of the floatplane. Skiers are borne to the tops of otherwise inaccessible mountains by helicopter or ski plane pilots, so they can ski down over miles of virgin snow. Single-engine aircraft tow gliders up three thousand or four thousand feet above ground level and release them to soar in the empyrean. Sport parachutists are taken aloft; then they jump out and aim for ground targets. Many pilots are employed by corporations to fly executives and business trips.

There are also many very small airlines, operating a few one- or two-engine planes to island resorts, offshore gambling havens, camps in the woods, and other places where there is a continuous but small stream of travellers. As an example, Scenic Airlines in Las Vegas flies tourists on a sightseeing trip to the Grand Canyon, lands them on the rim for a ground tour, and flies them back to Las Vegas at sunset. In such an operation, the pilot may conduct the ground tour, pick up the passengers from their hotels, and also perform the aircraft maintenance. He or she has considerable independence when airborne, but much less support from the ground than has the pilot of a commercial airline.

The actual minute-by-minute supervision of the aircraft in flight is not much work anymore. Whereas early pilots sometimes navigated by following highways and were lost when they got into fog, the modern pilot has all the advantages of radar and loran, radio compass, and many other helpful instruments. In addition, airline flight is monitored from the ground by flight controllers, who can advise pilots of the plane's precise position and warn about weather difficulties ahead, other aircraft in the path, or dangerously low altitude.

The pilot of past years controlled the plane's course constantly with a joystick; however, modern transport aircraft the flown mechanically during most of the flight, except during takeoff and landing. On most long flights, a minor compass correction once or twice an hour is about all that is needed to keep the aircraft in straight and level flight and on the shortest safe course to its destination. A computer makes all the tiny corrections that used to be made by a pilot's sensitive fingers on the joystick. But the pilot, copilot, and usually the flight engineer must be able to take control and fly the aircraft in any sort of emergency that might develop—from minor turbulence, to losing an engine, to diving the plane down to a safe altitude if the cabin is ruptured and depressurised.

Most of the pilot's skill and ability are never used, but are held in reserve in case of need. For people who want continual challenge to which they can respond vigorously, this kind of work can be frustrating. An airline pilot does not have the exciting fight against fate and elements that Charles Lindbergh had. Instead he or she spends long hours just keeping an eye on things.

At the beginning and end of every flight, however, the pilot earns that high pay by lifting the monstrous machine into the air and bringing it safely back to earth. The pilot often is called the captain by the airlines. Like the captain of a ship, he or she has total responsibility for the safety of passengers, crew and cargo. In the air, all passengers, as well as the flight crew, are subject to her or his orders. The copilot often is called first officer by the airlines, and the flight engineer second officer. In most airlines the captain wears four sleeve stripes, the first officer three, and the flight engineer two.

Work schedules are irregular, since they are based on when the majority of people want to fly. Vacationers typically want to fly on weekends and during non-business hours. Airline pilots, on average, are away from home bases overnight about one-third of the time. Airlines provide them hotel rooms and expense allowances for this.

The Federal Aviation Act forbids airline pilots and copilots to fly more than 100 hours per month or 1,000 hours per year. Most of them fly about 5 hours a month, but total hours on duty, including layover time before return flights, usually rise to 120.

Most pilots and copilots enjoy liberal vacations and other fringe benefits, including a considerable amount of free or law-cost personal travel. Joining an airline's cockpit crew is difficult, and keeping the job is challenging, but the responsibility, pay and prestige make it well worthwhile.

More and more women are becoming pilots, gaining experience, and flying hours as flying instructors and air-taxi pilots. In 2001 there were approximately 35,776 women pilots (students, private, commercial, airline transport and other). The fact that the airlines prefer pilots with military training has made it difficult for women to break in, but as the military services admit more women to their flight programmes, more women will also become airline pilots. (To find out more about female pilots, see the Sources of Information section at the end of this chapter.)

Flight Engineer

The flight engineer's job combines the fields of operations and maintenance of the aircraft. He or she is expected to be able to take over as captain of the plane if the pilot and copilot should in some way become disabled. Promotion to copilot comes after two to seven years and to pilot after five to fifteen years, in accordance with seniority and union contract.

New large aircraft have flight-management computers that do much of the flight engineer's work, so when they can safely do so, the airlines get along without flight engineers.

The main practical operating responsibility of the flight engineer is to know every blade and bolt and valve, every spark plug, transistor, wire, pipe, and tank on the aircraft. The flight engineer's place in the cockpit is well supplied with instruments that report on every critical point and phase of engine operation, electronic systems, fuel and its flow, temperature, and many other conditions.

When any instrument or combination of instruments shows something unusual, the flight engineer must be able to diagnose trouble rapidly, report it immediately to the pilot, and, if possible, repair it during the flight or arrange for removal of stress from an affected part until mechanics on the ground can repair it. If the next stop is at a small airport without mechanics trained for the particular type of aircraft, the flight engineer may well be the one to make the repair.

On a typical flight, the flight engineer joins the pilot and copilot in the preflight weather briefing and conference on route and altitude. Together they check the aircraft's maintenance record to be sure that needed overhauls and equipment replacement have been made as required. Arriving at the airplane, they inspect the exterior briefly, including the tires.

The flight engineer officer assists the pilot and copilot in making preflight checks of equipment, controls and instruments in the cockpit. He or she checks fuel levels, electric power, and engine-report instruments. In flight, the flight engineer adjusts controls to keep the engines at maximum efficiency, records engine performance and fuel consumption at frequent intervals, and watches cabin pressure and temperature and adjusts them as necessary.

Requirements

There are four level of pilot certificates: student, private, commercial and air transport (U.S. terminology) or airline transport (Canadian terminology). We will address the last three categories.

All airline pilots must pass extensive physical health requirements. In the United States, medical certificates required by the Federal Aviation Administration (FAA) are categorised as first, second, or third class. In Canada, Transport Canada has category 1 or category 3 certificates. Each class or category has specific requirements, which are valid for varying lengths of time.

The minimum age for private pilot certification is seventeen years. The pilot must hold a valid third-class (U.S.) or category 3 (Canada) medical certificate. In addition to a basic education, he or she must have specialised instruction in areas such as aviation regulations, navigation, radio communications, weather observation and evaluation, aircraft loading, and flight planning; and must pass an FAA written examination and demonstration of flight planning and manoeuvering.

For commercial pilot certification, the minimum age is eighteen years. The pilot must hold a valid and current second-class (U.S.) or category 1 (Canada) medical certificate. In addition to the education requirements of a private licence, a pilot must have extensive aeronautical experience. This includes at least 250 hours of flight time (in Canada, 200 hours), plus a minimum of 100 hours as pilot-in-command, 50 hours of cross-country (20 hours in Canada), 10 hours of instrument instruction, and an instrument rating (in Canada an instrument rating is not required, but an applicant must have 20 hours of instrument time). For certification, the commercial pilot must pass a more stringent written examination and demonstration of FAA procedures than does a private pilot.

For air transport pilot certification, the minimum age is twenty-three years. The air transport pilot must hold a current and valid first-class (U.S.) or category 1 (Canada) medical certificate. For the United States, 1,500 flight hours (night and cross-country included) plus instrument rating are required.

For Canada, a minimum of 1,500 flight hours (pilot-in-command and cross-country included) and a multi-engine rating in addition to an instrument rating are required. To be certified, air transport pilots must pass a more stringent written examination and demonstration of FAA procedures than do private or commercial pilots.

According to the FAA's Title 14 Code of Federal Regulations (CFR), Part 121—commonly known as the Age 60 Rule—a pilot may not engage in what are known as Part 121 operations if the pilot has reached are sixty. Part 121 covers scheduled passenger operations using multi-engine jet aircraft, scheduled passenger operations with multi-engine propeller airplanes that have a passenger seat configuration of ten or more seats, and common carriage operations of all-cargo airplanes that have a payload capacity of seventy-five hundred pounds or more. Pilots have been contesting the Age 60 Rule for years now.

For flight engineers, the same physical and height and weight standards are required by the airlines as for pilots and copilots—and the same coolness under fire. A flight engineer must be a high school graduate (some airlines require college as well) and must hold a valid and current second-class medical certificate in the United States. He or she is also required to have at least one of three aircraft ratings on the flight engineer certification as appropriate.

Education and Training

The armed forces have traditionally been an important source of training for many civilian pilots. Persons without armed forces training may become pilots by attending flight school. Most airlines require at least two years of college and prefer to hire college graduates.

As wars slip into history and time passes, the number of aviators with military training decreases. The FAA has certified some six hundred civilian flying schools to compensate for this. Among these are some colleges and universities that offer degree credit for pilot training. Airlines still prefer militarily trained pilots, but now they must also accept those with civilian training. The United States military has lost so many trained pilots to civilian work that it is hoping to curb this high attrition rate through special pay and bonuses. This will make the airlines more dependent upon civilian-trained aviators or on their own training for pilots and copilots.

Competition has been quite intense. Most of the candidates seeking employment possess a bachelor's degree and have jet or turboprop training and experience. Typically, they have well in excess of fifteen hundred total flight hours.

The major airlines strongly suggest getting a bachelor's degree, then joining the Air Force, Navy, Marines, or Army for flight training.

This is true throughout the airline industry. Learning to fly in a civilian flying school is possible but costly, and it could be difficult to acquire the fifteen hundred hours of flight time required for the transport licence. In time of war, when the military is using all the pilots it can get, the airline industry would no doubt take new pilots with minimum qualifications or even less than minimum. But during times of peace, when there are thousands of pilots looking for flying jobs, the airlines can take their pick, and they naturally choose the most highly qualified.

A sample description for a pilot's job with a major airline reads something like this.:

> The minimum qualifications required for pilot are, being at least twenty-one years of age and a graduate of a four-year degree programme from a college or university accredited by a recognised accrediting organisation. Postgraduate education will be given favourable consideration. Applicants should currently hold an FAA commercial fixed-wing pilot licence with an instrument rating; currently hold a valid FAA second-officer written exam (FEB and FEJ or FEX); and.have a minimum of.1,200.hours of total.documented flight time with a minimum of 1,000 hours of fixed-wing turboprop or turbofan time. Applicants invited to interview must provide appropriate documentation of all flight hours and possess a current FAA First Class Medical Certificate and be able to pass a medical examination. Part of the pre-employment screening process with require applicants to take a test to determine the presence (without a prescription) in the applicant's system of any substance that is controlled in the United States. Applicants must be able to pass a criminal and background check in order to qualify for unrestricted

access to security identification display areas; possess a valid passport or other travel documents enabling the bearer to freely exit and re-enter the United States (multiple re-entry status); and be legally eligible to work in the United States (possess proper working documents).

Before being allowed to take up passengers, the newly hired flight engineer, copilot, or pilot is given extensive training by the airline. This includes classroom instruction in meteorology, FAA regulations, and company policies and rules. Three to ten weeks of flight instruction consisting of lectures, time in simulated aircraft, and actual flights may also be given. A trainee who does not have a rating for the type of airplane he or she will be flying must earn it.

Very few people are hired to start as pilot/captain for the major airlines. Historically, most began as second officers, with eventual promotion to first officer and finally to captain. Nowadays, however, as second officers are being replaced by new technology, one's first job on the flight deck is as first officer. Reaction time and ability to make rapid correct judgments under stress are tested, and cockpit crew members must maintain excellent physical condition to keep their jobs.

Safe flying is the major ability demanded by airlines of their pilots. Punctuality for on-time departures and arrivals also is desirable, but safety is always paramount. Heroes are really not desired in this job. Airlines prefer steady, eminently well-qualified people who take pride in their own perfectionism as they check out equipment, weather, and all the many items that might possibly go wrong and cause trouble during flight. In addition to being a perfectionist, a pilot must be cool in emergencies. Previous flying experience, often in the military, will probably have subjected the pilot to many emergencies, perhaps in combat, where her or his mettle was tested and proved.

The best way for flight engineers to obtain the necessary training is in the armed forces, just as for pilots and copilots. A FAA flight engineer licence is required. Qualification for this consists of three or more year of experience as a pilot or second officer in the armed forces, or in repair and overhaul of aircraft engines. A stiff flight physical examination and a written test on engine operation and the theory of flight are also required for this licence, plus a flight check in an aircraft of the type to which the engineer seeks assignment. As applicant without armed services experience can study for the licence at a private aviation school approved by the FAA. Also required is the commercial pilot's licence.

Earnings and Job Outlook

In 2000, the average salary for airline pilots, copilots and flight engineers was $110,940. According to a September 2001 report from the Air Lines Pilots Association, International (ALPA), which represents sixty-six thousand airline pilots from United States and Canadian airlines, ALPA captains earned an average of $150,000. ALPA copilots earned an average of $93,000 annually. For airlines that do not fly aircraft requiring three crew members in the cockpit, the starting salary for a copilot ranged from $17,500 to $50,000 annually. ALPA flight engineers earned an average of $85,000 annually, and entry-level salaries ranged from $36,000 to $50,000.

Airline pilots and copilots earn more than those employed by corporations or government. More than half of U.S. airline pilots are members of a union. Most who fly for one of the major airlines belong to the Air Line Pilots Association, International. The union representing Air Canada's pilots is the Canadian Air Line Pilots Association. Pilot pay is decided upon by bargaining between union and company.

The Bureau of Labour Statistics reported that 94,820 pilots were employed in 2000. Air travel is very sensitive to economic swings, however, and a recession always causes reduction in numbers of flights and consequent crew layoffs. Restructuring of airlines in the 1990s and the events of 11th September, 2001, have reduced the need for pilots.

According to the Bureau of Labour Statistics, jobs for pilots, copilots and flight engineers are expected to increase by 6.4 per cent between 2000 and 2010. (This estimate was made prior to 11th September, 2001, when many pilots, copilots and flight attendants were furloughed.)

Aircraft Mechanics

One way in which a person can prepare to become a flight engineer is to first become an aircraft mechanic. There are almost twice as many aircraft mechanics as there are pilots, copilots and flight engineers combined. Although the travelling public seldom sees aircraft mechanics, there would be no flying without them.

In 2000, 173,000 aircraft mechanics were employed in the United States. Approximately 70 per cent of all salaried mechanics worked for airlines or airports and flying fields, about 12 per cent worked for the federal government, and about 9 per cent worked for aircraft assembly firms. Many of the remaining mechanics worked in general aviation, usually for independent repair shops. Many who work for the aircraft assembly firms are in California or Washington state. FAA facilities are in Oklahoma City; Atlanta; Wichita; or Washington, D. C. An airline usually operates a major repair base for each type of aircraft in its system.

Job Responsibilities

There are three main specialties among aircraft mechanics: power plant, airframe and avionics technicians. Avionics technicians work on instruments and propellers. Airframe mechanics are qualified to work on wings, fuselages and landing gear, while power plant mechanics work on engines.

In addition to doing such routine preventive maintenance as changing engine oil, greasing wheel bearings, and replacing spark plugs, aircraft mechanics dismantle engines check all the parts for wear, and rebuild them. The FAA requires regular inspection of airframes and power plants. When a flight is delayed for emergency repairs, mechanics must work fast to get the plane back into the air.

Education and Training

Training for most mechanics consists of graduation from high school or vocational school, plus some experience in a machine shop or auto repair shop. Major airlines operate apprenticeship programmes of three or four years' duration, combining classroom and on-the-job training. Those who have been aircraft mechanics in the armed forces can complete their apprenticeship rapidly. Or, if they are fortunate enough to have worked with aircraft very similar to those the airline flies, they might step right into a mechanic's job. The FAA has a list of mechanic schools that it has approved, and it will make the list available to anyone who is interested. Programmes at most of these schools are of one and a half to two years' duration.

Graduates of these schools, or mechanics with eighteen months of experience, are eligible to take the written and practical tests for a licence as an airframe or power plant mechanic or as an avionics repair specialist (A & P specialist). A mechanic trying for both airframe and power plant licences at once must have thirty months of experience. A mechanic who has had both licences for at least three years may take examinations and be qualified as an aircraft inspector, after which he or she certifies the work of other mechanics.

Licenced mechanics advance with increasing seniority and ability to lead. A mechanic may become a crew chief, shop foreman, maintenance supervisor, and perhaps company executive. Some start their own shops and work on contract for small airlines, corporations, government agencies, or other general aviation aircraft operators. Others learn to fly well enough to earn a commercial pilot's license and become flight engineers.

Earnings and Job Outlook

The airlines paid aircraft and service technicians an average of $19.50 an hour in 2000. Avionics technicians were paid an average of 19.86 per hour. Mechanics who are employed by the major airlines generally earn more than those working on other types of aircraft do. In addition, aircraft mechanics and technicians with FAA certification earn on average more than $4.00 per hour over those who are not FAA-certified.

Free or law-cost travel on the mechanic's own and other airlines, plus other fringe benefits, are standard.

Unions representing aircraft mechanics include the International Association of Machinists and Aerospace Workers, the Transport Workers Union of America, and the International Brotherhood of Teamsters.

Although employment of aircraft mechanics is expected to rise with the average for all occupations through the year 2010, it may be restricted as consolidation in the aircraft industry continues and more and more automated systems take on tasks for repair and replacement in aircraft. According to the Bureau of Labour Statistics, jobs for aircraft mechanics are expected to increase by 16.7 per cent between 2000 and 2010.

Air Traffic Controllers

The FAA was the employer of twenty-seven thousand air traffic controllers in 2000. Most air traffic controllers are stationed in the towers at major airports, at en route centers along established airways, or at flight service stations near large cities. Some work for the United Stated Department of Defence.

Heavy responsibility puts air traffic controllers under great stress, so anyone entering this kind of work should be prepared to cope with extremes of tension over long hours. Controllers may retire on pension after twenty to twenty-five years—a recognition of the strain they undergo. Mandatory retirement is at fifty-six years of age, and the National Air Traffic Controllers Association estimates half of the nation's controllers will retire by 2010, necessitating the hiring of new controllers to fill the positions.

Job Responsibilities

There are three types of air traffic control specialists (ATCS)—the terminal (or tower) controller, en route center controller and the flight-service station controller—and their main responsibility is to ensure the safe, orderly flow of air traffic. The terminal controller's main responsibility is to organise the flow of aircraft in and out of the airport. The en route controller takes over when an aircraft leaves an airport, directing pilots through their designated airspace. A flight-service specialist provides pilots with flight and in-flight weather information, suggested routes, and other important flight information.

Education and Training

Applicants for American controller duties must be U.S. citizens, younger than thirty-one years of age, have vision correctable to

20/20, and have clear, precise diction. Many controllers come from the armed forces, while many others are trained by FAA-certified colleges with degrees in aviation administration with an emphasis in air traffic control. Applicants usually must have three years of general work experience or four years of college or a combination of both. The United States Office of Personnel Management gives competitive examinations in major American cities.

Chosen applicants are given eleven to sixteen weeks of classroom and on-the-job training at the FAA Air Traffic Academy in Oklahoma City. They learn aircraft performance characteristics, aviation regulations, the airways system, and controller equipment, and receive intensive training in flight simulators. Full qualification as a controller takes three to six years. Every controller is given a physical examination once a year and a job performance review twice a year. Controllers can advance to chief controller, regional controller, and to administrative positions in the FAA.

Control towers never close down, so controllers must work frequent night shifts on a rotating basis. In addition to their forty-hour workweek, they may work extra hours for overtime pay or compensatory time off.

Earnings and Job Outlook

According to the Bureau of Labour Statistics, the average annual salary in 2000 was $53,313. The middle 50 per cent earned between $62,250 and $101,570, the lowest 10 per cent earned less than $44,760, and the highest 10 per cent earned more than $111,150. The government gives thirteen to twenty-six paid vocation days and thirteen days of sick leave annually. Controllers, salaries are determined by collective bargaining contracts. The trade union is the National Air Traffic Controllers Association.

According to the Bureau of Labour Statistics, jobs for air traffic controllers are expected to increase by 7.2 per cent between 2000 and 2010.

Further information and application forms are available from the U.S. Office of Personnel Management (see the Sources of Information section at the end of this chapter), which also administers the written test.

Aviation Safety Inspectors

The FAA is responsible for the safety of almost every facet of aviation, including certification of aircraft, pilots, mechanics and people involved in manufacturing aircraft. In 2001 U.S. aviation was serving more than 622 million passengers, a number expected to rise to one billion by 2013, according to the FAA.

Job Responsibilities

Aviation safety inspectors administer and enforce safety regulations and standards for the production, operation, maintenance, and/or modification of aircraft used in civil aviation. There are eight different types of FAA inspectors, including (1–3) general aviation avionics/maintenance/operations inspectors; (4–6) air carrier avionics/maintenance/operations inspectors; (7) manufacturing inspectors; and (8) cabin inspectors.

Requirements

Experience is the primary requirement for an inspector's job. For example, candidates for a manufacturing inspector position must have experience in the area of quality control/quality assurance systems, methods, and the techniques in the manufacture of aircraft, aircraft engines, propellers, or class II products. This experience should demonstrate their ability to determine that aircraft and related products meet the approved design criteria and are in condition for safe operation. They may also have responsibility for the issuance of original airworthiness certificates or original expert airworthiness approvals for aircraft, aircraft engines, propellers and class II products.

Avionics, maintenance, operations and manufacturing inspectors are hired primarily from a national registry or pool of qualified applications. An application must be filled out, and an applicant is notified if he or she is eligible for an inspector position. For cabin safety inspectors, if a vacancy is available, it is posted on the FAA Career Opportunities website (see the Sources of Information section at the end of this chapter).

Earnings and Job Outlook

U.S. Aviation Safety Inspector (ASI) earnings are classified according to the General Schedule (GS) pay tables and range form GS-9 (2002 tables: $43,365) to GS-15 (2002 tables: $104.604). Current GS pay tables can be obtained from the U.S. Office of Personnel Management (OPM) website. (See the Sources of Information section at the end of this chapter). Earnings in the Washington, D.C., headquarters area generally range from GS-12 to GS-15.

The FAA continues to look for people who are technically proficient with the emerging aviation technologies, have strong business systems management skills, and are competent in the use and application of information technology.

Reservation and Transportation Agents and Travel Clerks

In 2000, according to the Bureau of Labour Statistics, 126,000 people held jobs as reservation and transportation agents and travel clerks in their transportation industry.

Job Responsibilities

Reservation agents and clerks for major airlines and large hotel chains generally work in central offices. As the human link between the telephone and a computer terminal, the agent gives information on flight schedules and the availability of seats and makes reservations. Agents receive calls from the general public, from travel agents, and form their own company's ticket agents. They generally do not come face-to-face with customers, but do all their contact work by telephone.

Transportation agents, sometimes known as passenger service agents, passenger-booking clerks, reservations clerks, airport service agents, or ticket clerks, work at ticket counters in airports and in central-city ticket offices. They answer questions about fares and schedules, give out timetables and descriptive literature, check directly with computers or with reservation agents for seat availability, and sell tickets, often by typing the passengers' names into the computer. Fares are so complicated in air travel that selling a ticket is a more difficult procedure than it might seem. Ticket agents check in and tag baggage, add any excess-baggage charges, and issue boarding passes to permit passengers to get to the airplanes. Passenger agents help airport ticket agents, help passengers board the aircraft, collect tickets, and in some cases assign seats. At some airlines, these personnel are called customer service clerks (entry level) and customer service agents.

Ticket and passenger agents are as smartly uniformed as flight crews. They are selected on the basis of pleasing personality and appearance, good diction and education. High school graduation generally is required, and two or more years of college are preferred. Chances for advancement are improved by college courses in traffic management and other phases of transportation.

Outside sales agents for the airlines often are called traffic representatives. They visit shippers and corporations, keeping present customers happy and trying to obtain new customers. Ticket and reservation agents may advance to supervisor in these specialties or to traffic representative.

Heading all sales efforts are city sales managers, and above them, district sales managers. The district sales manager administers ticket and reservations offices, directs the efforts of sales representatives, and promotes traffic on the airline.

Earnings and Job Outlook

According to the Bureau of Labour Statistics, the median hourly earnings for reservation and transportation agents and travel clerks in 2000 were $11,67. As automated reservations—such as "ticket-less" travel or kiosks to let passengers book their own flights—reduce the number of workers necessary, job outlook for these types of positions will not rise significantly. However, travel related positions can never be fully automated for security and safety reasons, and as travel grows and turnover in the industry occurs, there will be job openings.

According to the Bureau of Labour Statistics, jobs for reservation and transportation ticket agents and travel clerks are expected to increase by 14.5 per cent between 2000 and 2010.

Sources of Information

The many organisations associated with the airline industry have excellent sources of information, including up-to date job websites. Here are some:

Air Line Pilots Association, International (ALPA)
1625 Massachusetts Ave. NW
Washington, DC 20036-2283
alpa.org

Career information, including a list of accredited pilot schools in the United States and Canada, can be found at: alpa.org/internet/publications/cpb/carrer_pilot_brochure.pdf.

ALPA is a union representing sixty-six thousand airline pilots at forty-three U.S. and Canadian airlines. Founded in 1931, it is chartered by the AFL-CIO.

Air Transport Association, Inc. (ATA)
1301 Pennsylvania Ave. NW, # 1100
Washington, DC 20004
airlines.org.

ATA is the nation's largest airline trade association, accounting for 95 per cent of the passenger and cargo traffic carried by U.S. scheduled airlines.

Association of Flight Attendants, AFL-CIO (AFA)
1275 K St. NW
Washington, DC 2005
afanet.org

Career information is available at: afanet.org/airline_job_links.htm. AFA is the world's largest labour union organised by flight attendants for flight attendants. It represents more than fifty thousand flight attendants at twenty-six airlines.

Aviation Inforamtion Resources, Inc. (AIR, Inc.)
3800 Camp Creek Pkwy., Ste. 18-100
Atlanta, GA 30331
airapps.com

AIR is dedicated to providing complete, timely and accurate information to help pilots make informed decisions throughout their job search and to assist them in their career development as airline pilots.

Federal Aviation Administration (FAA)
U.S. Department of Transportation
800 Independence Ave. SW
Washington, DC 20591
faa.gov.

FAA Aviation Education Career Guides: faa.gov/education/rlib/career.htm

FAA approved air traffic controller schools: faa.gov/education/rlib/arc.htm

FAA Air Traffic Academy website: atctrining.faa.gov/site

International Flight Engineers' Organisation (IFEO)
IFALPA Headquaters
Interpilot House
Chertsey, UK KT169AP
ifalpa.org

IFEO was formed in 1992 by the merger of the Flight Engineers' International Association (FEIA) and the European Flight Engineers Organisation (EFEO). It is now the only international organisation for flight engineers.

International Society of Women Airline Pilots (ISA+21)
2250-E Tropicana Ave., Ste. 19-395
Las Vegas, NV 89119-6594
iswap.org

ISA+21 is an educational and charitable non-profit organisation that seeks to stimulate and encourage women to enter the airline pilot workforce as active cockpit crew via education and scholarship.

National Air Traffic Controllers Association (NATCA)
1325 Massachusetts Ave.
Washington, DC 20005
natca.org

NATCA ensures the safety and longevity of air traffic controller positions around the nation.

The Ninety-Nines, Inc.
International Organisation of Women Pilots
International Headquarters
Box 965, 7100 Terminal Dr.
Oklahoma City, OK 73159-0965
ninety-nines.org.

The Ninety-Nines is an international organisation of licenced women pilots from thirty-five countries and has more than sixty-five hundred members worldwide.

Professional Aviation Maintenance Association (PAMA)
Ronald Reagan Washington National Airport
Washington, DC 20001
pama.org.

PAMA's mission is to enhance professionalism and recognition of the aviation maintenance technician through communication, education, representation, and support for continuous improvement in aviation safety.

Transport Canada
Department of Transport
330 Sparks St.
Ottawa, ON
Canada K1A 0N5
tc.gc.ca

Transport Canada works to help ensure Canadians the best transportation system by developing and administering policies, regulations, and programmes for a safe, efficient, and environmentally friendly transportation system.

Universal Pilot Application Service (UPAS)
P.O. Box 550010
Ft. Lauderdale, FL 33355-0010
upas.com

U.S. Bureau of Labour Statistics (BLS)
U.S. Department of Labour
2 Massachusetts Ave. NE
Washington, DC 20212-0001
bls.gov

U.S. Bureau of Transportation Statistics (BTS)
U.S. Department of Tansportation
400 Seventh St. SW
Washington, DC 20590
bts.gov

U.S. Department of Transportation (DOT)
400 Seventh St. SW
Washington, DC 20590
dot.gov

U.S. Office of Personnel Management (OPM)
1900 E St. NW
Washington, DC 20415-0001
opm.gov
Job openings. usajobs.opm.gov
GS pay tables: opm.gov/oca/02tables/indexgs.htm

This is the human resources agency of the U.S. government.

3

CRUISE LINES, RAILROADS, BUS LINES AND TOURISM

The airline industry has grown to be a gigantic industry in the last tow decades, overshadowing other modes of travel such as boat, rail and bus. However, there are many places that airplanes cannot get to, and the alternative method of getting there would be by railroad and bus. Travel by boat—including cruise ships, car and passenger ferries, excursion and dinner boats, and gaming vessels—is expanding in the United States as the demand for waterborne recreation grows and federal, state and local governments find ways to ease congestion on highways and roads. There are many job opportunities for those interested in working in the travel industry in these fields. This chapter includes information on the historical background, job responsibilities, training, earnings, and job outlook and information resources of the cruise, rail and bus industries.

Cruise Lines

According to the Cruise Lines International Association (CLIA), the cruise industry is the fastest-growing segment of the travel industry—achieving more than 1,400 per cent growth since 1970, when approximately 500,000 people took a cruise. It is estimated that by 2002, 7.4 million people will have taken a cruise.

The North American cruise industry's growth is also reflected in the significant increase in passenger capacity. In the 1990s, nearly eighty new ships were introduced, and over the next five years, the cruise industry will introduce at least fifty two new ships. Furthermore, in North America, only 12.3 per cent of the population has ever taken a cruise, and polls suggest that over 50 per cent would like to.

About two-thirds of the world's cruise trade is generated in the North American market, but most cruise-ship officers are European, while most crew members are European, West Indian or Asian.

The cruise industry is an important part of the U.S. travel industry. According to a study conducted by Business Research and Economic Advisors (BREA) and Wharton Econometric Forecasting Association (WEFA), the cruise industry contributed some $17.9 billion to the U.S. economy in 2000 and generated 257,000 full-time jobs for U.S. citizens.

There are few American cruise ships or freighters. The United States Merchant Marine has been in sad straits for years because of the cost American labour, both for building ships and for staffing them. Costs are three or four times what ship owners in Europe and Asia pay. As a consequence, U.S. shipping survives only when heavily subsidised by the government or when heavy defence spending for military or aid ventures brings employment to American ships. Congress in 1970 agreed to subsidise the construction of thirty new ships per year until 1980. This vigorous construction programme was intended to revitalise American shipping, but in actual practice, older ships were retired or scrapped at the same rate new one were built.

Many U.S. shipping companies register their ships in Panama, Liberia, and other countries where they can pay low taxes and avoid high labour rates. Americans can work on these ships, but at low rates of pay. Also, having worked on a ship flying a "flag of convenience," an American may have a difficult time later getting a job on an American-flag ship, because a U.S. union might refuse membership.

Passenger transportation across the oceans has been taken over almost completely by the airlines, and the great passenger liners have been retired or adapted to the cruise trade. Cruising has been gaining rapidly in popularity, and it is the salvation of the passenger ship. Many new cruise ships were built in the

1980s, and about twenty were under construction in 1995. New York City, formerly the departure point for about one hundred cruises to the Caribbean every winter, built a new passenger ship terminal in 1974. Fly-cruise packages had been introduced, however, giving the passenger a flight to meet a ship in Miami or a Caribbean port : this gradually ended winter cruises from New York. But as more and more people discovered the delights of the cruise, the cruise seasons became a year-round industry in the Caribbean.

From New York City, beginning in the mid-1980s, some three hundred cruises departed annually during warm weather, sailing to Bermuda, the Bahamas, Canada, and all around the Caribbean. Cruises up the inland waterway to Alaska and from West Coast ports to Mexico, Central and South America, and the Caribbean are also increasing their sailings and bookings. Fly-cruise packages now also take North Americans to join their ships in the Mediterranean, in Hawaii, and in the Orient.

Job Responsibilities

If you think of a cruise ship as a ship, hotel, theater, entertainmen center, sports center, wellness spa, restaurant, bar, shopping mall and many other types of businesses combined, you can imagin the varying types of jobs on board. Job titles range fron beautician, cashier, and cruise or recreation director to nurse anc doctor. Bartender, purser, and tour staff are popular jobs, bu oftentimes one must start out as a room steward (or stewardess and work up to waiter, bartender, or office staff.

Careers at sea in the "water transportation industry" are stil possible for Americans on American- or foreign-flag ships anc even in the United States passenger trade. According to th Bureau of Labour Statistics, there were 70,000 wate transportation workers in 2000. This figure includes 32,00 sailor and marine oliers, 25,000 ship and boat captains an operators, and 8,600 ship engineers.

Shipboard work is divided among three departments. Th deck department operates and navigates the ship, maintains th hull and deck equipment, and supervises loading, storing an unloading of cargo. The engine department operates an maintains the propulsive machinery. And finally, the steward's department feeds the crew and passengers and cleans the living spaces.

Education and Training

It is possible to become captain of a ship with no formal education. The catch is that there are many Coast Guard examinations to take to qualify for the licences that are necessary to advance. The person with no educational background is up against severe competition from graduates of the one federal and six state merchant marine academies.

To do it the hard way, one would obtain seaman's papers from the Coast Guard, wait in a union hiring hall until shipped out as an ordinary seaman, after a year take examinations to become an able seaman, after three years at sea take examinations for third mate, and at annual intervals take examinations for second mate and master status. However, this progression would take many years, and even with master's papers, the seaman might not always become captain of a ship.

A more likely path to advancement is graduation form the United States Merchant Marine Academy at Kings Point, New York, or one of the six state maritime academies. Like the service academies, entrance to the United States Merchant Marine Academy is by congressional appointment and College Entrance Board examinations. Students are paid a small allowance, and their education is free. The second year is spent at sea aboard an American commercial ship. Each graduate receives a Bachelor of Science degree, a license as third mate or third assistant engineer, and an ensign's commission in the United States Naval Reserve. Almost without exception, this is the course followed by prospective ship captains today. The law requires that graduates of the Merchant Marine Academy must serve at least five years in the merchant marine or the military.

The Merchant Marine Academy places nearly all its graduates in seagoing jobs before they graduate. Merchant marine officers' careers from that point depend upon their doing a good job, studying for examinations for second mate and master, and taking the exams as early s possible. After this, they simply must work and wait for a captain's job.

The six state academies are: California Maritime Academy at Vallejo; Maine Maritime Academy at Castine; Massachusetts Maritime Academy at Buzzards Bay; Texas Maritime Academy at Galveston; New York Maritime College at Fort Schuyler, New York City; and Great Lakes Maritime Academy at Traverse City, Michigan. All these schools charge tuition. Contact the Office of Maritime Labour and Training (see the Sources of Information following this section) for a list of the state maritime academies and the link to the United States Merchant Marine Academy.

People in the steward's department generally work up from unskilled jobs such as mess attendant and utility hand to third cook, second cook (the ship's baker), and chief cook. Above the chief cook is the chief steward. The chief steward is not a ship's officer, but nevertheless is answerable to the captain. On a passenger ship the steward's department is by far the largest, employing many waiters and room stewards.

When doing job research, it's wise to determine the nationality of the ship's crew. Often it is difficult to get an engine room or desk job unless you are the same nationality as the ship's officers. Most ship's officers are Norwegian, Greek, or Italian, with a handful of British and American ships. In addition, many of the technical crew jobs in the engine room or on deck are staffed with Filipinos.

It is best to go directly to the cruise lines when seeking employment for a position other than captain, ship engineer, or sailor. For a list of all cruise ships' mailing and website addresses, log on to the Cruise Lines International Association (CLIA) or the International Council of Cruise Lines (ICCL) websites listed in the Sources of Information at the end of this section.

Earnings and Job Outlook

According to the Bureau of Labour Statistics in 2000, water transportation earnings varied considerably by position and experience, from minimum wage to $33.77 per hour for a ship engineer position. Median hourly earnings for ship or boat captains and operators were $21.62; ship engineers, $22. 85;

sailor and marine oilers, $13.52; and all other types of positions, $11.70.

Shipboard personnel receive free room and board, so they are able to save most of their earnings if they can withstand the temptations of the ports they visit. Premium rates are paid for overtime. Officers generally can earn about 50 per cent above base pay for overtime and extra responsibilities. There are numerous strong unions covering most seafaring jobs.

In a 2000 cruise market study by the Cruise Lines International Association, it was found that the existing cumulative market potential over the next five years could be as high as $ 85 billion, creating the need for personnel growth. According to the Bureau of Labour Statistics, jobs for ship and boat captains and operators are expected to increase by 3.4 per cent between 2000 and 2010 and 5.8 per cent for ship engineers.

Sources of Information

Canadian Merchant Service Guild
218 Blue Mountain St., Ste. 310
Coquitlam, BC
Canada V3K 4H2

Cruise Lines International Association (CLIA)
500 Fifth Ave., Ste. 1407
New York, NY 10110
cruising.org

CLIA is the official trade organisation of the North American cruise industry.

International Council of Cruise Lines (ICCL)
2111 Wilson Blvd., 8th Fl.
Arlington, VA 22201
iccl.org.

The ICLL's mission is to participate in the regulatory and policy development process and promote all measures that foster a safe, secure and healthy cruise ship environment.

International Organisation of Masters, Mates and Pilots
700 Maritime Blvd.
Linthicum Heights, MD 21090
bridgedeck.org.

Marine Engineer's Beneficial Association
444 N. Capitol St., Ste. 800
Washington DC 20001
d1meba.org.

Office of Maritime Labour and Training
Maritime Administration
U.S. Department of Transportation
400 Seventh St. SW
Washington, DC 20590
marad.dot.gov.

Paul Hall Center of Maritime Training and Education
P.O. Box 75
Piney Point, MD 20674-0075
seafarers.org/phc.

Seafarers' International Union of North America
5201 Auth Way
Camp Springs, MD 20746
seafarers.org.

U.S. Coast Guard National Maritime Center
Licencing and Evaluation Branch
4200 Wilson Blvd., Ste. 630
Arlington, VA 22203-1804
uscg.mil/stcw/m-pers.htm.

Railroads

Following World War II, the airlines gradually took over most of the long-haul domestic passenger traffic that traditionally had belonged to the railroads. Service on many lines became so poor that it seemed the railroads were trying to get rid of passengers. As new population centers developed, there were many places not served by rail, and no new rail lines were laid. Intercity bus service improved and carried most of those passengers who did not fly or use their own cars. By 1970, railroads were accounting for only 1 per cent of intercity passenger miles.

A new chapter in railroad history began when the National Railroad Passenger Corporation (Amtrak)—a quasi-public corporation dedicated to providing modern, efficient, attractive service—began operating the nation's passenger railroads on 1st, May, 1971. Amtrak was started just in time. It finally had been admitted that automobiles were a prime cause of air pollution and that individual transportation would have to be reduced by improving mass transportation, which causes less pollution. Then came the energy crisis of the winter of 1973-74, reinforced in the spring of 1979, which jolted Americans into realising that a really severe shortage of gasoline could force them to use mass transportation.

There were many growing pains as Amtrak strove to meet rapidly increasing demands. New types of trains were designed and built, many cars were bought, and a nationwide computerised ticketing and reservation system was installed and operating in 1974. Many of the roadbeds were in poor repair, and introduction of high-speed trains was pointless until the roadbeds were improved. Amtrak improved the New York—Washington tracks so that fast metroliners could travel at 110 miles per hour. An investment that has paid off splendidly is America's first high-speed train, the Acela Express, in the Northeast corridor. It is now constantly full with passengers, it cost less than $3 billion all told, and, as of this date; it is operating in the black. Washington and Oregon are spending state money to build a high-speed corridor between Seattle and Portland. In Chicago, a liberal non-profit law firm is spearheading a nine-state high-speed effort for the Midwest United States.

Amtrak has been very heavily subsidised by congressional appropriations since its inception. In 1979 Congress mandated that Amtrak be able to pay its own way by the end of 2002, which it has not been able to do. Amtrak asked for a loan of $205 million in short-term financial help, threatening to shut down the passenger rail lines and the commuter lines that use its tracks at the end of June 2002. Negotiations took place in the summer of 2002. Legislators were leaning toward liquidating Amtrak and returning the rails to private service. However, just as the deadline was approaching, Congress agreed once more to bail out Amtrak. To date, Amtrak's financial problems are not yet resolved.

Canada's rail history has been similar to that of the United States, with passengers leaving the railroads to drive their own cars, and equipment and tracks sinking into poor condition. Equipment and maintenance improvements have been made, but at high cost. The Canadian government contributed $597 million for 1983 expenses in excess of revenue. The ongoing improvements the Canadian Rail System (VIA) achieved over the past decade continued in 2001. Revenue increased by $13 million, bringing total revenue growth over the last three years to more than $50 million. Passenger numbers increased by seventy thousand and yield—the measure of revenue earned per passenger mile—increased by approximately 6 per cent. Despite higher fuel costs, total operating costs were lower than anticipated. As a result, VIA was able to reduce its requirement for government operating funding by another $7 million. And for the first time in VIA's history, the ratio of revenues over cash operating expenses exceeded 60 per cent to reach 61.5 per cent.

The U.S. Department of Labour noted 531,000 railroaders working in 1976, 433,000 in 1982 and 115,000 in 2000. Railroad jobs, as expected, continued declining at a rate of 1.8 per cent a year.

Job Responsibilities

There are a number of important jobs involved in rail travel. They include the following:

Clerks

Clerks are the largest group of railroad employees. They work in railroad stations, company offices, yards, terminals, and freight houses. Most railroads require a high school education and may require applicants to take a clerical aptitude test. Some clerical training or experience also is beneficial. Most clerks belong to the Transportation Communications International Union. Railroad clerks can advance in many directions—to cashier, executive secretary, accountant, statistician, chief clerk, auditor, ticket agent, station agent, buyer, or supervisor. Both men and women have found opportunities in this area.

All passenger rail systems, including Amtrak, utilise a nationwide computerised reservation system, an innovation in passenger railroading. Most passengers now get information through computerised telephone lines and can book their own reservations online. This has resulted in the decrease in the number of clerks needed to handle reservations and information.

Conductors

The conductor is in charge of the train, whether it carries freight or passengers. He or she signals the engineer when to start, and can order a stop for any emergency. Passenger-train conductors collect tickets and money and furnish schedule and fare information.

Conductors are usually male and are promoted from the job of brake operator, which used to be called brakeman or trainman. Passenger-service brake operators attend to car lighting and temperature and may help collect tickets. Many women are now passenger-service brake operators, and many of them will become conductors.

Conductors, brake operators, and all train-crew personnel often work irregular hours, including nights and weekends, getting premium pay for overtime. Most brake operators and conductors belong to the United Transportation Union.

Engineers and Brake Operators

Locomotive engineers drive great machines powered by diesel engines or electricity. They are the most experience and skilled workers on the railroad. A few people are hired specifically for training to become engineers; most are promoted from brake operator positions after passing examinations.

Newly hired brake operators should be between the ages of twenty-one and thirty-five, with a high school education and excellent hearing, eyesight, colour vision and hand-eye coordination.

The new brake operator is trained on-the-job by the engineers with whom he or she rides and is given a regular assignment when one becomes available. Within a year of being hired, the helper starts a six-month engineer-training course, which is composed of both formal instruction and on-the-job training. He or she must pass numerous tests to qualify as an engineer, and then may have to wait several years until there is a vacancy. In passenger service, brake operators are often called assistant conductors.

Shift work is common in over-the-road work and in local lines and yards.

Storing Agents

Station agents in small stations sell tickets, check baggage, compute express and freight charges, and may direct the operation of some trains. In progressively larger stations, the station agent is a supervisor of these activities or an administrator of a large staff.

Station agents usually are promoted from the ranks of railroad clerks, telegraphers, telephoners, and tower operators. Those in the last three groups direct the movement of trains from towers in terminals and yards. To be hired, they should be high school graduates and have excellent hearing, eyesight, colour vision and diction.

Amtrak wants its employees to advance and has a programme to provide educational assistance for employees who want to take job-related courses of study. There is also a very liberal pass policy at Amtrak and on most non-passenger railroad lines. Amtrak employees have unlimited free transportation on a space-available basis, excluding certain special high-fare trains. Employees' spouses and dependents are given twelve free trips a year and as many more as they desire at half fare.

Earnings and Job Outlook

According to the Bureau of Labour Statistics, median hourly earnings of locomotive engineers were $21.26 in 2000; railroad conductors and yardmasters, $18.86; railroad brake, signal and switch operators, $18.82; and rail yard engineers, dinkey operators and hostlers, $17.69.

Most railroad workers in road service are paid according to miles travelled or hours worked, whichever leads to higher earnings. Full-time employees have steadier work, more regular hours, increased opportunities for overtime work, and higher earnings than do those assigned to the "extra" board.

According to the National Railroad Labour Conference (NRLC), in 1999 the average annual earnings for Class I railroad engineers ranged from $61,400 for yard-freight engineers to $81,000 for passenger engineers. For conductors, earnings ringed from $53,500 for yard-freight conductors up to $68,300 for passenger conductors. The NRLC reported that brake operators averaged form $40,800 for yard-freight operators up to $58,700 for local-freight operators.

According to data from the American Public Transportation Association, in early 2001 the top-rate full-time hourly earnings of operators for commuter rail ranged from $17.50 to $30.10; operators for heavy rail from $16.20 to $27.70; and operators for light rail from $14.40 to $23.90. Transit workers in the northeastern United States typically had the highest wages.

Nearly 80 per cent of railroad transportation workers are members of unions. May different railroad unions represent various crafts on the railroads. Most railroad engineers are members of the Brotherhood of Locomotive Engineers, while most other railroad transportation workers are members of the United Transportation Union. Many subway operators are members of the Amalgamated Transit Union while others belong to the Transport Workers Union of North America.

According to the Bureau of Labour Statistics, jobs in railroad transportation are expected to decrease approximately 18.5 per cent between 2000 and 2010.

Sources of Information

More information on salaries, job openings, and job specifications is available from any railroad for which you may want to work or from any of the thirteen unions with which Amtrak has bargaining agreements. You may with to contact any of the following:

Amtrak
60 Massachusetts Ave. NE
Washington, DC 20002
amtrak.com

Association of American Railroads (AAR)
50 F St. NW
Washington, DC 20001-1564
aar.org

AAR is one of the nation's oldest and most respected trade associations, representing the major freight railroads of the United States, Canada and Mexico.

Brotherhood of Locomotive Engineers (BLE)
1370 Ontario St., Mezzanine
Cleveland, OH 44113
ble.org

BLE is North America's oldest rail labour union, with more than thirty-five thousand active members in the United States and Canada.

Federal Railroad Administration
400 Seventh St. SW
Washington, DC 20590
fra.dot.gov.

United Transportation Union (UTU)
14600 Detroit Ave.
Cleveland, OH 44107-4250
uut.org (United states)
utu-canada.org (Canada)

The UTU is a broad-based transportation labour union representing about 125,000 active and retired railroad, bus and mass transit workers in the United States and Canada.

Bus Lines

The United States has a magnificent infrastructure to support bus line: 3,857,356 miles of public roads and streets, including 42,500 miles on the unparalleled interstate highways system.

What a change has taken place since stagecoaches on rudimentary trails were replaced by intercity buses! The first such bus route was established in Oregon, between Bend and Shaniko, in 1905. Early buses, which had solid tires and no springs, were exceedingly uncomfortable and often broke down. Drivers had to be innovative mechanics, but even with the best of efforts a bus sometimes had to be towed home by borrowed team of horses.

With today's miles of excellent roads, buses can go almost anywhere is the United States and southern Canada, including large areas not served by airlines or trains. If stronger efforts are made to reduce dependence on private cars, thus helping alleviate both air pollution and fuel expenditure, the use of buses will increase.

The modern intercity bus provides not only transportation, but also large windows and sometimes an upper deck for viewing the scenery. Most also offer air conditioning, rest rooms, and comfortable reclining seats, in addition to a high degree of reliability in meeting schedules and an exceedingly low accident rate. Buses used especially for sightseeing may have tour guides, who point out interesting sights in passing and lead the passengers when they disembark to visit a particular area. Thus, buses are an important and growing segment of the travel scene.

Deregulation of the bus industry in the early 1980s spawned fifteen hundred new bus companies, many of them small but determined to succeed. Greyhound Lines, Inc., the major nationwide intercity bus operator, controls the majority of American buses. Greyhound Lines in a single corporation. It started in 1914 with a two-mile run for fifteen cents in an open, seven-passenger car, between the Minnesota towns of Hibbing and Alice. In 1987 Greyhound purchased Continental Trailways, its major competitor, and absorbed the Trailways system within its own. Greyhound Lines, Inc., now serves more than twenty-six hundred destinations with eighteen thousand daily departures across the country, and in 2000 it carried more than nineteen million passengers. It currently has approximately five thousand drivers, is based in eighty-eight locations across the country, and employs more than thirteen thousand workers. The company's busiest route is New York to Atlantic City, with well over two thousand passengers travelling between these locations daily. New York to Washington, D. C., is second, with an average of thirteen hundred passengers on the route each day.

Another major bus operator in the travel field is Gray Line Sight-Seeing Companies Associated, Inc., founded in the United States in 1910. This corporation of 150 independently owned long-distance and local sightseeing tour companies is widely recognised and respected as the world's largest sightseeing tour company, serving more than two hundred destinations worldwide. Inquiries about jobs with a Gray Line company can be made to one of its numerous member companies around the world.

Bus drivers held approximately 666,000 jobs in 2000.

Job Responsibilities

Millions of Americans every day leave the driving to bus drivers. Bus drivers are essential in providing passengers with an alternative to their automobiles or other forms of transportation. Motor-coach drivers transport passengers on charter trips and sightseeing tours. Drivers routinely interact with customers and tour guides to make the trip as comfortable and informative as possible. As with all drivers who drive across state or national boundaries, motor-coach drivers must comply with U.S. Department of Transportation regulations. Tour and charter bus drivers may work any day and all hours of the day, including weekends and holidays. Their hours are dictated by the charter trips booked and the schedule and prearranged itinerary of tours. However, like all bus drivers, their weekly hours must be consistent with the Department of Transportation's rules and regulations concerning hours of service. For example, a long-distance driver may not work more than sixty hours in any seven-day period, and drivers must rest eight hours for every ten hours of driving.

Job Requirements

Bus driver qualifications and standards are established by state and federal regulations. All drivers must comply with federal regulations and any state regulations that exceed federal requirements. To qualify for a commercial driver's licence, applicants must pass a written test on rules and regulations and then demonstrate they can operate a bus safely. A national data bank permanently records all driving violations incurred by persons who hold commercial licences. All drivers must be able to read and speak English well enough to read road signs, prepare reports, and communicate with law enforcement officers and the public. In addition, drivers must take a written examination on the Motor Carrier Safety Regulations of the U.S. Department of Transportation.

Many employers prefer high school graduates and require a written test of ability to follow complex bus schedules. Many intercity and public transit bus companies prefer applicants who are at least twenty-four years of age; some require several years of bus or truck driving experience. Because bus drivers deal with passengers, they must be courteous. They need an even temperament and emotional stability, because driving in heavy, fast-moving, or stop-and-go traffic and dealing with passengers can be stressful. Drivers must have very strong customer service abilities, including communication skills and the ability to coordinate and manage large groups of people.

Earnings and Job Outlook

Median hourly earnings of transit and intercity bus drivers were $12.36 in 2000.

The benefits bus drivers receive from their employers vary greatly. Most intercity and local transit bus drivers receive paid health and life insurance, sick leave, and free bus rides on any of the regular routes of their line or system. Drivers who work full-time also get as many as four weeks of vacation annually.

Persons seeking jobs as bus drivers throughout this decade should encounter good opportunities, especially those individuals who have good driving records and who are willing to start with a part-time or irregular schedule.

Local and intercity bus travel is expected to increase as the population and labour force grows. Consequently, employment of local transit and intercity drivers will increase to accommodate the greater number of riders. However, more individual travellers will opt to travel by airplane or automobile rather than by bus. Most growth in intercity drivers will probably be in group charter travel, rather than scheduled intercity bus services.

Most intercity and many local transit bus drivers are members of the Amalgamated Transit Union. Local transit bus drivers in New York City and several other large cities belong to the Transport Workers Union of America. Some drivers belong to the United Transportation Union and the International Brotherhood of Teamsters.

According to the Bureau of Labour Statistics, jobs for school, transit and intercity bus drivers are expected to increase by 13.2 per cent between 2000 and 2010.

Sources of Information

American Bus Association (ABA)
1100 New York Ave. NW, Ste. 1050
Washington, DC 20005-3934
buses.org

The ABA is the trade association of the intercity bus industry.

American Public Transportation Association (APTA)
1666 K St. NW
Washington, DC 2006
Apta.com

APTA members serve the public interest by providing safe, efficient, and economical transit services and by improving those services to meet national energy environmental and financial concerns.

Bureau of Labour Statistics
U.S. Department of Labour
2 Massachusetts Ave. NE
Washington, DC 20212-0001
http://stats.bls.gov/oco/ocos242.htm

Canadian Bus Association
451 Daly Ave.
Ottawa, ON
Canada K1N 6H6
buscanada.ca

Gray Line Worldwide
Gray Line House
1835 Gaylord St.
Denver, CO 80206
grayline.com

Greyhound Lines, Inc.
P.O. Box 660362
Dallas, TX 75266-0362
greyhound.com

4

HOTELS, MOTELS AND RESORTS FOR TOURISTS

Throughout history, whenever it was safe to travel, there have been places of public accommodation. In Asia and Asia Minor today, there are small inns called *khans* that provide shelter only. The Bible mentions that the sons of Jacob, returning from Egypt, stopped at such an inn and fed their animals. It was a khan in Bethlehem where Joseph and Mary found no room and had to go to the stables, where Christ was born. Out on the roads, usually at wells, *caravansaries*—huge stone forts large enough to hold one or several caravans with all their animals and strong enough to defend them against attack by bandits—were built at regular intervals. These can still be seen, particularly in Turkey.

Ancient Persians built luxurious inns along their fine road system, as did ancient Romans. When the Romans conquered Britain, they introduced the *taberna* for drinking and the *caupona* for overnight accommodations. During the Dark Ages, travel was possible only by groups that could defend themselves, like small armies. The Knights Hospitallers built many hospices for Crusaders and pilgrims to the Holy Land in the twelfth century, and in western Europe from this time on, abbeys often served as inns—some still do. In England there were about six thousand inns along the high roads and coach routes in the 1500s. Caravansaries had been spaced about eight miles apart, and English inns were fifteen miles apart, showing that a day's journey now covered twice as much distance. The Industrial

Revolution spawned railroads, and the resulting increase in travel caused construction of large city hotels. Spa resorts soon followed.

The first known hotel in North America was the Jamestown Inn, built in 1607, the year the colonists arrived in Virginia. A postal service commenced in 1710, after which inns multiplied along the post roads. Resort hotels began opening at eastern U.S. health spas in the 1700s and on the seashore in the 1800s. Large hotels were built around city railroad stations, and as pioneers pushed westward, a hotel was often the first building in a new settlement.

The automobile caused construction of the first "tourist cabins," which later developed into motels. Travel increased with automobiles, and later with aircraft, and hotels proliferated around the world. Several international airlines built hotels in distant, exotic places to provide lodging for their passengers. The industry includes all types of lodging, from upscale hotels to campgrounds, spas, inns and boardinghouses.

Hotels and motels make up the majority of lodgings. There are also four basic types of hotels—commercial, resort, residential and extended-stay. The majority of motels and hotels are in the transient or commercial category, and the number of resort hotels is growing rapidly as more people take vacations. About 10 per cent of U.S. hotels are residential, meaning that they rent or lease their rooms for long periods to permanent or semipermanent residents. Extended-stay lodging combines the features of a resort and of a residential hotel. Rooms are much like furnished apartments. For example, they have fully equipped kitchens, computer and telephone hook-ups and so forth. Usually these rooms are used for a minimum of five consecutive nights.

According to the American Hotel and Lodging Association, in 2000 there were fifty-three thousand properties, 4.1 million rooms, $108.5 billion in sales, and an average occupancy rate of 63.7 per cent.

Bricks and mortar provide only part of what the weary traveller wants. Most of the remainder is service, which means people working to fill every request. Out of every dollar taken in by hotels and motels, thirty cents are spent for employees' wages and fringe benefits and the cost of their meals.

Advancement is likely to be faster and further for those who enter the hotel business with an education. There are usually openings at several different entry levels in hotels, with opportunities to advance in various parts of the business.

Many resort hotels used to be open only one season each year. Employees might work in a resort in the Catskill Mountains in New York in summer and in Florida hotel in winter. Now, however, northern summer hotels are using skiing and other sports to attract a winter clientele, and Florida hotels stay open all year, reducing their rates during the summer.

Many a hotel or motel worker advances by saving money until he or she can set up an independent business. According to the Bureau of Labour Statistics, in 2000 there were approximately sixty-eight thousand hotel managers and assistant managers working for wages or salaries and an additional number of self-employed owners of motels and small hotels.

Job Responsibilities

Modern hotels offer much more than rooms and meals for travellers. The variety of services they provide adds to the number and types of hotel jobs. Besides guest rooms and restaurants, a hotel may have special bars or nightclubs; banquet facilities; meeting rooms with audiovisual and translation equipment; large ballrooms; sales exhibit rooms; swimming pools; marinas, golf courses, or tennis courts; ski tows and lifts; travel agencies; beauty and barber shops; valet services; airline offices; theater ticket agencies; newsstands; gift shops; baby-sitting services; car, boat and plane rentals; health clubs; stage and film theaters; and gambling casinos. Today, many hotels offer cutting-edge technology to accomplish state-of-the-art meetings and conventions. They have on-site information technology staff, any number of means to connect to the Internet and videoconferencing capabilities.

A large hotel may have six major departments and some auxiliary ones. The executive department may include a general manager, resident manager, controllers or accountants, management trainees, and directors of sales, personnel, rooms, food and beverages, housekeeping and public relations.

In the front office are people directly responsible for personal contact with the guests. These include mail clerks, room clerks, reservation clerks and the front-office manager. The accounting department has auditors, bookkeepers, office-machine operators, cashiers and other clerical workers responsible for handling the operation of the business.

The housekeeping department includes the housekeeper, housekeeper's assistants, heavy-cleaning people, seamstresses, tailors, launderers, decorators, upholsterers and others. Redcaps, valets, elevator operators, and door people work under the superintendent of service in the service department. They are responsible for maintaining a near and clean home for visitors.

The restaurant department has chefs, cooks of various grades and types; kitchen helpers, a steward and staff, pantry keepers, storeroom employees, dishwashers, food servers, bartenders, bus people and other food and beverage service workers.

The maintenance department has stationary engineers to operate machinery for heating and air-conditioning guest rooms and public rooms, and for cooling large refrigerators. This department also employs electricians, plumbers, carpenters, painters and locksmiths.

Front-office Workers

Front-office clerks do much of the hotel's minute-by-minute business with guests. The room clerks rent rooms and greet guests, assign rooms, sell various services, open billing records for new guests, advise housekeepers of arrivals and departures and keep reservations lists. When a room is assigned, the desk clerk turns the key over to a bell person who takes the guest to the room.

Reservation clerks receive reservations in person or by mail, fax, telephone, or Internet, and acknowledge them. They type out registration forms and advice room clerks of each day's list of arriving guests. Reservations for hotel and motel rooms are now mostly done over the Internet so that a traveller has instant confirmation of a reservation.

Mail and information clerks place mail, messages, and keys in guests' boxes and give these out when called for. They answer telephones and route incoming calls to the right rooms. They also may sell stamps and advise guests about transportation, attractions and events.

Most of North America's elegant hotels now have a concierge sitting at a prominent desk in the lobby. This is often a personally young woman or man who speaks several languages. The functions of the concierge are many and varied. He or she provides guests with all sorts of information; arranges reservations or tickets for dinner, the theater, airlines, tours, sports facilities, or events; arranges introductions; lends umbrellas when it rains; and solves any guest room problems of heat, cold, humidity, plumbing, or other inconvenience. The symbol of the concierge is crossed keys on the lapels. The position and the term *concierge,* long common in Europe, become widespread in North American luxury hotels in the 1980s.

The front-office manager supervises all these functions, coordinates the actions of the front-office with those of the housekeeper and others, schedules work shifts and assignments of clerks, inspects rooms periodically, and handles the many kinds of complaints and problems that can arise in a hotel. Most front-offices never close, so if clerks fail to arrive, the manager must find substitutes or fill in for the absent clerk.

Cashiers keep track of guest charges, total them when a guest leaves or at regular intervals and accept payment. Accountants bill guests regularly, handle the hotel's payroll, and prepare regular profit-and-loss statements.

For the person who is ambitious for success in the hotel business, the front-office is the place to learn all about hotels and how to cope with all the problems that can arise. Inexperienced newcomers usually fill openings for beginners' clerical jobs in the front office. Sometimes bell people, switchboard operators, or other employees who appear capable are promoted to such jobs.

Education and Training

Educational requirements for front-office jobs vary according to the type and size of hotel, its location, and its own standards. A high school education in desirable. Graduates of two or four-year colleges often start as management trainees, rotating from one department to another, but obtaining major experience in the front-office. Even better for such a carrier is graduation from two-or four-year course in hotel and motel management. These specialised curricula are becoming widespread as colleges realise the growing importance of the lodging industry. (See the Appendix for a list of U.S. schools.)

It is still possible for a person without a high school education, but with a good personality and native ability and intelligence, to rise to the top in the lodging business. Such advancement becomes more difficult, however as college-trained people enter the business as management trainees. So it makes sense to obtain the best education you can. In addition to more rapid advancement, the person with greater education is generally paid more in top management positions.

If you want to enter the lodging business directly after high school, try to attend a technical high school offering hotel-related courses. Courses that might be beneficial include cooking, business administration, management and economics.

For its employees who have little or no education, the hotel industry provides training courses. In New York City, for example, the Hotel Association, in cooperation with the Hotel and Motel Trades Council, AFL-CIO, operates its Industry Training Programme. Free fifteen-week courses that combine classroom and on-the-job training are given at various hours to accommodate people on different shifts. Courses include English, basic accounting, repairs and maintenance, food and beverage control, floor housekeeping, telephone switchboard operation, night auditing, business machine operation, typing and front-office procedures. There are similar programmes in many cities. Many hotel workers who started as maids or busboys have profited by these courses to become housekeepers, cashiers, auditors and room clerks among other higher-level jobs.

High schools in many cities have adult education programmes with specific courses for hotel workers. Some large hotels and chains have their own in-house schools, combining formal classes with on-the-job training.

An industry educational programme applicable to a variety of situations is that of the Educational Institute of the American Hotel and Lodging Association (AH & LA-EI). (See the Sources of Information section at the end of his chapter for contact information.) These courses can be taken by mail on an individual basis, in small groups without an instructor, in larger groups with instructors, or through cooperating colleges that teach institute courses, as well as online courses. Courses cover many topics, from the basics of sanitation and bookkeeping on up to marketing and hotel/motel property management. People can take single courses in a special-interest subject, such as food and beverage operations, or take ten courses and earn the Institute's diploma. Beyond this, by taking five courses in advanced management, having five years of industry experience, and demonstrating service to the industry, a hotel worker can earn distinction as a certified hotel administrator.

Earnings and Job Outlook

Employment at hotels, motels and resorts has advantages and disadvantages. There is always room for advancement for the hard worker who is willing to study and learn. Work in the lodging industry offers variety. When a person reaches the top in a small operation, he or she can generally move to a larger one and keep advancing. A person with a good record can usually find work in any part of the travelled world, and certainly in any part of the United States or Canada. Hotel workers in a chain usually can vacation in the chain's various properties at a fraction of the regular fee.

Bus person and housekeeper wages are low, but job security is good and meals and uniforms are often provided, so that the cost of living is reduced.

At the middle-management level, salaries are good compared to these in other industries, and at top management levels, the salaries can be very high. Hours worked per week are comparable with those in other industries, but many jobs must be performed at night, on Sundays, and on holidays, which can disrupt social or family life.

The following table from the Bureau of Labour Statistics shows the median hourly earnings in the year 2000 of the largest occupations in hotels and other lodging places.

Occupations	*Hotels/Motels*
Lodging managers	$14.95
Maintenance and repair workers, general	9.98
Cooks, restaurant	9.96
Security guards	9.61
Hotel, motel and resort desk clerks	7.84
Laundry and dry-cleaning workers	7.48
Maids and housekeeping cleaners	7.09
Baggage porters and bellhops	6.74
Waiters and waitresses	6.60
Gaming dealers	6.26

The Bureau of Labour Statistics predicts that wage and salary employment in hotels and other lodging places will increase 13 per cent between 2000 and 2010, slower than the 16 per cent growth projected for all industries combined. This growth reflects rising personal income, an increase in the number of two-income families, low-cost airfares, emphasis on leisure activities, and growth of foreign tourism in the United States. In addition, special packages for short vacations and weekend travel should stimulate employment growth. As more states legalise some form of gambling, the hotel industry will invest in gaming.

Job opportunities should be concentrated in the largest hotel occupations, such as building cleaning workers and hotel, motel, and resort desk clerks. Many of these openings will be in resorts, spas and full-service hotels.

Employment outlook varies by occupation. Employment of hotel, motel and resort desk clerks is expected to grow rapidly as some of these move up to managerial positions. However, the spread of computer technology will cause employment of other clerical workers, such as bookkeepers, accountants, and auditing clerks and secretaries, to grow more slowly than the industry as a whole. Employment of waiters and waitresses will no doubt decline since the trend is for hotels and other lodging places not to offer full-service restaurants.

The employment of lodging managers is expected to increase more slowly than that within the overall hotel industry since the economy-class establishments will have fewer departments to manage. However, the trend toward chain-affiliated lodging places should provide managers with opportunities for advancement into general manager positions and corporate administrative jobs. Jobs for lodging managers are expected to increase by 9.3 per cent between 2000 and 2010.

Job turnover is high in this industry. To attract and retain workers, the lodging industry is placing more emphasis on hiring and training.

Sources of Information

For information on various careers in hotels, motels and resorts, contact the following:

Hospitality Careers

American Hotel and Lodging Association (AH & LA)
1201 New York Ave. NW, Ste. 600
Washington, DC 20005-3931
ahlaonline.org

AH & LA is a ninety-two-year-old federation of state lodging associations throughout the United States with some thirteen thousand property members worldwide, representing more than 1.7 million guest rooms. Its website has links to hospitality schools, hospitality-related associations, lodging industry trade press, and state hotel and lodging associations.

American Hotel and Lodging Educational Foundation (AH & LEF)
1201 New York Ave. NW, Ste. 600
Washington, DC 20005-3931
ahlf.org

AH & LEF provides financial support that enhances the stability, prosperity, and growth of the lodging industry through educational and research programmes.

Educational Institute of the American Hotel and Lodging Association (AH & LA-EI)
800 N. Magnolia Ave., Ste.1800
Orlando, FL 32803
ei-ahma.org

AH & LA-EI is the premier source for providing industry-tested, research-driven, hospitality training resources worldwide.

International Council on Hotel, Restaurant and Institutional Education (I-CHRIE)
2305 Skipwith Rd.
Richmond, VA 23294-4442
chrie.org

I-CHRIE is the global advocate of hospitality and tourism education for schools, colleges and universities offering programmes in hotel and restaurant management, food-service management and culinary arts.

Food and Beverage Service

American Culinary Federation, Inc. (ACF)
10 San Bartola Dr.
St. Augustine, FL 32086
acfchefs.org

ACF is a professional, not-for-profit organisation for chefs and cooks. Its goal is to promote the professional image of American chefs worldwide through education among culinarians at all levels, from apprentices to the most accomplished certified master chefs. Contact the ACF for information about apprenticeship and certification programmes for cooks.

National Restaurant Association
1200 Seventeenth St. NW
Washington, DC 20036-3097
restaurant.org

The National Restaurant Association is the leading business association for the restaurant industry. Together with the National Restaurant Association Educational Foundation, the association's mission is to represent, educate and promote a rapidly growing industry that is comprised of 858,000 restaurant and food-service outlets employing 11.3 million people.

Housekeeping and Janitorial

Service Employees International Union (SEIU)
1313 L St. NW
Washington, DC 20005
seiu.org

The Service Employees International Union is made up of 1.5 million working service employees and 120,000 retirees united to improve their jobs and communities.

Housekeeping Management

International Executive Housekeepers Association (IEHA)
1001 Eastwind Dr., Ste. 301
Westerville, OH 43081
ieha.org

The IEHA is a professional and educational organisation of approximately six thousand members involved in or directly affiliated with the various facilities management and allied professions.

5

TRAVEL AGENCIES FOR TOURISM

Today travel agencies are deeply concerned that their customers will start dealing directly with hotels and carriers *via* the Internet, bypassing the agencies. Thirty-nine per cent of travellers who go online think the Internet is easier and faster to use for travel planning than is a travel agent, according to the "Yesawich, Pepperdine & Brown and Yankelovich Partners' 2002 National Travel Monitor" report. In addition, the expansion of electronic ticketing—not to mention airlines cutting back on agency commissions, passenger fear of air travel, and the economic situation—make travel agent employment a slow growth travel occupation.

However, many consumers still find the process of booking a vacation on their own cumbersome and time-consuming and prefer to hire a professional travel agent to ensure a good holiday at a good price. The 2002 National Travel Monitor also states that although use of the Internet for researching and booking travel arrangements is higher than in previous years, three out of every ten leisure travellers still use the services of a travel agent. Travel agents responsibilities are concerned more with adding value to leisure or corporate travel itineraries rather than actually booking the trip.

According to the Bureau of Labour Statistics, travel agents in 2000 held 135,000 jobs, and more than eight out of ten salaried agents worked for travel agencies. The remainder worked for other travel organisations.

History

Ticket agencies have existed since ancient Rome, when postal employees sold tickets for the use of chariots and roads and made out an *itinerarium*—the ancestor of the modern traveller's itinerary. Operators of packet boats, stagecoaches, trams, railways, and steamships sold tickets in their offices for rides on their equipment.

Thomas Cook, a printer in England, started the business of the general travel agency; that is, the selling of tickets and tours that utilised the facilities of other companies. Railroads had just commenced operation, and Cook, an ardent non-drinker, wanted to use them to advance the temperance cause. In 1844, he chartered a train to carry people from Loughborough to Leicester, where they would attend a temperance convention and return. Charging twenty-five cents each, he crowded 541 people aboard this first special train—the first round-trip ticket in history.

Cook operated other temperance tours that were very popular. He soon realised that people were more attracted by travel at low prices than by temperance, so he began operating tours for entertainment, education and other purposes. Ten years after his first tour, 165,000 people used his transportation and lodging arrangements to visit a great fair at the Crystal Palace in London. Cook opened a London office in 1865, by which time he was already sending tours to Europe and the Holy Land. In 1866 he led the first escorted American pleasure tour, visiting cities such as New York; Washington, D.C.; Richmond; Cincinnati; Toronto; and Montreal; and sites including Civil War battlefields, Mammoth Cave, and Niagara Falls. In 1872 he led a tour of twenty-two-people around the world. His son John M. Cook promoted the firm in America and other places outside Britain. In 1974, Cook introduced what were called *circular notes.* In a slightly different form, these became known as traveller's checks, which today are issued by Cook's, American Express, and several of the major North American and European banks.

American Express, another major travel agency, was established in 1850 with the merger of the firms of Henry Wells and William G. Fargo, who also organised Wells Fargo two years later. Initially American Express was a shipping concern, but it moved into banking and tourist services and by 1918 was out of the freight business.

Cook's, American Express, and a number of other large agencies organise and operate their own tours, as well as sell tickets for all kinds of travel. They also make individual travel arrangements, and some agencies specialise in certain national destinations to which they send frequent charter tours. Others arrange trips for youth groups, ski enthusiasts and other particular interest groups.

Today

Most travel agencies do not organise tours themselves. Instead, they are in the business of selling trips and tours that are offered by travel wholesalers and carriers. As of June 2002, the American Society of Travel Agents (ASTA) estimated there are about twenty-seven thousand travel agency locations (including branches) in the United States. Some of these are operated solely by the owner; however, the average agency has five or six full-time and one or two part-time employees.

Travel agents give out a tremendous amount of advice and information to prospective travellers, but they make no money unless they sell tickets and hotel reservations. Working for a travel agency, therefore, means selling; so a person not interested in selling should not enter the agency business. There are benefits to the travel agent's job—like free or inexpensive "familiarisation" trips by carriers and hotels—but the new employee is not likely to receive these. Low-cost air travel and hotel rooms are usually made available after a probationary period, but for the first few years, an agency employee might be able to use these only on her or his annual one- or two-week vacation.

Travel-agency employees need to be able to find specific information rapidly on all kinds of schedules, fares, special excursions, tour offerings, car rentals, guide services, seasonally varying hotel rates, and a host of other details. It usually takes many months for a new employee to become really useful in an agency, especially a small agency. In a vast concern like American Express, jobs are compartmentalised and easier to learn.

Job Responsibilities

An employee of a travel agency takes on quite a variety of tasks. She or he gives out travel literature about destinations; airline and cruise "packages" that cover almost all costs for transportation, accommodations, and meals; bus tours in the local area; and perhaps helicopter and train tours. The agent answers questions about comparative costs for accommodations and transportation as prospective travellers seek the last expensive or most luxurious vacations. She or he makes out itineraries that can be quite long and complicated if there are numerous stops and various hotels. When the client has approved a proposed itinerary, the agency clerk has to issue tickets and vouchers, sending copies to airlines and hotels to confirm reservations made by telephone, fax mail, or E-mail.

Travel agency personnel sell travellers' checks and special tickets such as Eurail passes; they also arrange for rental cars and escorted tours. By agreement with other travel agencies around the world, they can offer all kinds of local services in any city the traveller might reach.

Business in a travel agency changes from month to month, according to current attractions and time and money available to travellers. School and business vacations determine when many people take trips. The rich and the retired to south in winter and the energetic go skiing. Resort areas have high seasons and low seasons, and they are always trying to extend the high season a little longer with special attractions. For example, Atlantic City's Miss America contest was designed to add a week to the short summer season, and it has been successful at this for eight decades. Many places have notable annual events, such as Carneval in Rio de Janeiro, Mardi Gras in New Orleans, New Year's Eve in New York's Times Square, and Oktoberfest in Bavaria. For major world events such as the Olympic Games and for popular cruises, accommodations are booked well in advance.

Requests to an agency are changing constantly, and clerks must remain alert to new tours, excursions, special fare offerings, and constantly changing fares and schedules.

A large part of the agent's business is arranging travel and accommodations for business travellers. This, in fact, constituted the greater part of the travel business until the 1970s, when tourism became larger in gross billings than business travel. Some large corporations have their own in-house travel personnel to make direct bookings with carriers.

Requirements

Qualification to work in a travel agency varies widely from one office to another, and some agencies will accept people with less than a high school education. All, however, prefer applicants who have completed high school. College training, of course, enables one to move up faster and further. Beginners often start as administrative assistants. As they do the paperwork, they gradually learn about the business and can begin to answer inquiries and deal with the public.

For the student who hopes to enter a travel agency upon graduation from high school, valuable experience can be accumulated as a part-time employee working one or two hours per day on Saturdays or during summer vacations.

There is no federal licensing requirement for a travel agent. However, fourteen states have regulations that stipulate travel agents must have a licence to sell certain travel products. The website for the American Society of Travel Agents lists these states. For further information, contact your state's Office of the Attorney General or Department of Commerce.

Education and Training

Vocational schools offer six- to twelve-week travel agent programmes. Travel agent courses are offered in community colleges, four-year colleges, and adult education centers. In addition, there are bachelor's or master's degrees in travel and tourism. A list of U.S. schools by state can be found on the ASTA website.

For entry-level travel agents, the Institute of Certified Travels Agents. (ICTA) offers excellent books on a travel agent career, including the nation's leading travel and tourism textbook, *Travel Career Development,* 7the edition. This book is an authoritative, single-source text that provides the educational foundation students will need in the travel industry. (See the Sources of Information section at the end of this chapter for a list of books.)

The national TAP Test is a basic competency test that measures the entry-level knowledge of travel professionals within all aspects of the travel industry. ICTA, ASTA, and other industry partners developed the test to provide a national standard of excellence for the travel industry. The test is given on scheduled or open dates in selected cities in the United States.

The Certified Travel Associate (CTA) programme is ICTA's first level of certification and was introduced in 1997 to meet the needs of travel professionals in the early stages of their careers. The CTA programme focuses on the knowledge and the sales skills necessary for effective practice in the travel industry. It covers four core skill areas: communication and technology, geography, sales and service and the travel business itself. CTAs must possess eighteen months of full-time industry experience and are required to earn ten continuing education units each year to maintain their designation. The CTA programme represents 40 per cent of the study necessary for the CTC programme, and many CTAs go on to achieve their CTC designations.

The Certified Travel Counsellor (CTC) designation is the pinnacle of travel industry professionalism. The CTC curriculum covers three core skill areas: business development, contemporary issues and professional development. CTC candidates are required to complete twelve courses in which they learn how to negotiate effectively, make dynamic presentations, analyse new business opportunities, implement technological solutions, plan for the future, and more. The first level of ICTA certification, the CTA, must be successfully completed in order to earn the CTC designation. CTCs must possess at least five years of full-time travel industry experience and are required to earn ten continuing education credits each year to maintain their designation.

For the new employee in a travel agency, there are courses that help her or him learn the business much faster than would be possible by accumulated experience alone. ASTA provides five home study or online specialist courses, the cost of which is reduced if the student is a member of or employed by a member of ASTA. Costs cover instruction material, exams, evaluation and E-mail support. The course titles are Family Travel Specialist, Niche Travel Specialist, Mature Adult Travel Specialist, North American Rail Travel Specialist, and Travel Marketing Specialist.

One way to earn continuing education credits each year is to take one of ICTA's thirteen Destination Specialist (DS) courses. The Destination Specialist courses provide travel industry professionals with detailed knowledge of specific world areas, enabling them to match clients with the right travel products. Each course features destination highlights, sample itineraries and cultural insights. The thirteen programmes cover Africa, Alaska, the Caribbean, China, East Asia, Eastern Europe, European culture and heritage, Hawaii, Latin America, North America, the South Pacific, special-interest travel and Western Europe. Each DS course includes a comprehensive textbook with extensive maps, a world atlas, a practical study guide, and a job aid. Upon successful completion, ICTA will provide a diploma that states a country of specialisation.

ICTA offers educational workshops and featured speakers live *via* its online E-Learning Center. You can go online to view speakers discuss topics such as CTA Preparation or the Seven Habits of Highly Effective Travel Agents. Costs for these sessions are reduced for ICTA members.

ASTA Foundation, Inc., is a non-profit subsidiary of the American Society of Travel Agents. The foundation offers more than twenty scholarships for the most qualified students in a bachelor's, master's, doctoral, community college, or travel school programme, and to travel professionals seeking to further their education.

The Cruise Lines International Association (CLIA), headquartered in New York, represents nearly 95 per cent of the North American cruise industry. In 1993 CLIA introduced a major Cruise Counsellor Certification Programme, which provides travel agents with advanced courses that lead to an Accredited Cruise Counsellor (ACC) or Master Cruise Counsellor (MCC) designation. Credits are earned *via* a combination of classroom training, video training, Internet training, cruise experience, attendance at CLIA cosponsored conferences, ship inspections, CLIA Institute participation, completion of CLIA's new textbook, and case studies. Credit is also given for completion of CTA and CTC designations mentioned in preceding paragraphs.

Employment

How does one get a job in a travel agency? Jobs in online or in classified advertisement sections of newspapers generally are listed under the "Travel" heading. Most such advertisements demand experience in an agency or in similar work for an airline or other carrier or hotel. A newcomer in the field should search online or look for ads for "travel trainees," "travel entry level" positions, or for clerical, typists, assistants, or even messengers—anything to get inside an agency so you can start accumulating the necessary experience that helps qualify you for a better agency job. ASTA's website has a job bank that lets you select on the basis of job functions and location.

The trade press of the travel industry also carries advertisements for positions. Among the publications you should check for help wanted ads are *Travel Agent Magazine, Travel Weekly* and *Travelage West.* (See the Sources of Information section at the end of this chapter for websites.) These publication circulate only to travel agencies, but an agency will probably give you a few copies if you ask.

You can approach very large travel agencies directly any time because they must frequently hire trainees to replace other employees who have been promoted or moved. Corporate mergers of giant companies have occurred in the travel field as well as in most other industries. American Express purchased

Thomas Cook Travel and is now called American Express Travel Related Services, Inc. Carlson Travel Network merged with Wagon Lits Travel and is now called Carlson Wagonlit Travel. IVI Travel merged with U.S. Travel System and is now called World Travel BTI. These and Rosenbluth Travel are the top companies in business and corporate travel. Each of these companies has sales in the billions of dollars every year.

An agency usually rents or buys one of the Global Distribution Systems (GDS), which are computer reservations systems used by the industry. The major GDSs used in the United States today are Sabre, Amadeus, Worldspan and Galileo. A large agency might join two systems to avoid the "reservation bias" that can be built into any single system. Familiarity with at least one of these systems, plus knowledge of personal computers and their operating systems, can increase your salary by thousands of dollars in a travel agency; by the same token, computer illiteracy can stop you dead.

Travel positions are handled by personnel agencies, and there are a few travel-job specialists. Yours in Travel Personnel Agency, Inc. (aka Yours in Travel Groupes) was founded by P. Jason King in New York in 1972. Today, with branch locations in more than ten cities, Yours in Travel is the nation's largest recruitment source for the travel, tourism, transportation and hospitality industries. The company is also global, servicing four continents. Yours in Travel recruits personnel for many companies in the travel and tourism industries throughout North America and overseas. Salaries range from $20,000 for travel school graduates and for well-travelled beginners up to $500,000 for senior executives.

Earnings and Job Outlook

According to a 2000 survey conducted by *Travel Counsellor Magazine,* the median annual salary for a travel agent was $31,500, up 5 per cent from 1999. Eight per cent took home $60,000 or more, and 17 per cent earned less than $18,000. The size and type (leisure versus business) of the travel agency, experience of the agent, and the location all are determining factors of salaries.

Airline commissions—for both domestic and international tickets—make up a large portion of travel agency commissions. A big debate occurring now centers around commissions airlines pay to travel agents: in March 2002 the major airlines started the final round to reduce base commissions to zero, and some airlines continue to have performance-based programmes that pay override commissions. Car rental companies following in the footsteps of the airlines are eliminating agents' commissions for corporate rentals.

Commissions for travel arrangements, cruises, hotels, and sight seeing tours run about 7 to 10 per cent of the total sale. Rail commissions run about 5 per cent of the total sale. Approximately 29 per cent of travel agents receive compensation by salary alone, 15 per cent are paid commission only, and 56 per cent receive a combination of salary and commission and/or bonuses.

Travel agents more and more are charging fees for such non-commissionable services as obtaining visas for a traveller, sending faxes making long-distance telephone calls for last-minute reservations, and working out especially complicated itineraries. If a carefully planned trip is cancelled, an agent is likely to charge a planning fee.

A special type of travel wholesaler is the tour consolidator, who arranges the cheapest form of air travel—charter trips. There are usually no hotel or dining arrangements with such trips—only round-trip air transportation. The consolidator charters an airplane, or perhaps a block of seats, and sells transportation through advertisements or, more typically, to clubs or occupational groups that take care of the clerical work and collect the money for the trip. The work of the consolidator requires knowledge of airlines, a willingness to take risks, selling ability, and usually a fairly large amount of capital. One way to acquire the necessary skills in to work for a consolidator or in the charter department of an airline.

Just as in any other job, there are certain disadvantages associated with working for a travel agency or being a travel agent. The business is seasonal, making it necessary for some employees to be laid off for a part of every year. Most people consider pleasure travel a luxury; therefore, it is often one of the first things to be cut from the family budget when there is an economic downturn. Agents can cope with a minor economic downturn by scheduling clients for relatively inexpensive forms of travel, but in a very serious recession, travel agencies may be forced out of business.

For employees just starting in the travel agency business, there is a great deal of detail work, which some people do not enjoy. Travel agents also deal with the public constantly, and a few travellers—the haughty, supercilious, and demanding—are very hard to please. At peak seasons, a travel agent often must work long hours with constant interruptions by clients.

Despite the best efforts of travel agents, travel arrangements can be upset by such unexpected distant events as a strike of airline flight attendants in Iceland or of airline mechanics in Paris, or an earthquake in Nicaragua or Greece. The agent then must work frantically to save as much as possible of an itinerary and re-plan the rest.

Because of the allure of travel, many young people are attracted to jobs in travel agencies. By the law of supply and demand, large supply means low price; therefore, beginning personnel are not well paid. For this reason, personal travel is considered to be part of a travel agency employee's pay.

Examine your reasons for wanting to be a travel agency employee or owner. If the main attraction is personal travel, you may want to rethink the matter thoroughly. Could you earn higher pay in another industry and perhaps travel just as much? You would be paying for your travel, of course, but as a paid passenger, you would experience no waiting for hours for space-available seats, nor would you be bumped at the last minute just because one more ticket-holding passenger came aboard.

On the other hand, people who stick with an agency can advance to earning generous salaries, having time off when they want it, and getting the pick of their travel desires over most of the world. A travel agent can sometimes please clients best by pleasing herself or himself. F. C. M. Pauwels, a travel agent who operated the five-person Plaza Travel Service in New York, liked music and the Orient. So as part of his regular work, he led groups of music lovers on three or four-week tours of European music festivals and others on tours of the Orient.

According to the Bureau of Labour Statistics, jobs for travel agents are expected to increase by 3.2 per cent between 2000 and 2010.

Self-employment

Should you go into the travel-agency business yourself—as owner, owner manager, or partner? If you have the capital it is not difficult, because agencies are always for sale as owners retire or decide to sell for other reasons. If you are not experienced in the travel agency field, it would be much better to buy a partnership in a going business rather than buy a business outright and try to operate it from scratch.

What about the possibility of simply renting a store and putting up a sign to say that you're a travel agent? This probably would not work at all, since you would not be accredited to sell the tickets of the major carriers, and therefore, would have to buy tickets through another agent and split the commissions.

A growing number of professional travel agents choose to work from home, either as outside sales employees or independent contractors. Outside sales are compensated by commissions and independent contractors keep all the commission earned from sales, but they pay a fee to a travel agency that issues the tickets or provides them services. In both scenarios, when they build up enough capital, know-how, and familiarity with the accrediting agencies, they go into business for themselves. Other people have done the same sort of thing, starting by chartering buses for church and club outings and selling tickets—just as Thomas Cook did at the beginning of his business—and gradually working up to becoming travel wholesalers. The National Association of Commissioned Travel Agents, Inc. (NACTA) is the travel industry's leading association for independent travel agents, cruise-oriented agents, home-based travel agents, and outside-sales travel agents. Books on becoming a home based travel agent can be researched on the Internet using keywords such as "home based travel agent" or "spare time travel agent".

To be an agent of any kind, you have to represent one or more principals. A principal can be an airline, cruise line, or a purveyor of lodging, food, and other services. An agent can be appointed directly by a supplier, as is typical with hotels, car rental companies, and tour operators. The other way is to be appointed by a coordinating body accepted by various suppliers. The two coordinating bodies for the airlines are the Airlines Reporting Cooperation (ARC) and the International Airlines Travel Agency Network (IATAN). When an established agency is sold, the new owner must qualify for her or his appointments. For cruise lines, the coordinating body is the Cruise Line International Association (CLIA), and for trains it is Amtrak.

Sources of Information

Information on various travel agent-related organisations can be found by contacting the following:

Travel Agent Associations

American Society of Travel Agents (ASTA)
1101 King St., Ste. 200
Alexandria, VA 22314
asta.org

ASTA, primarily an association of travel agencies, is the major trade association for travel agents.

Association of Canadian Travel Agents
130 Albert St., Ste. 1705
Ottawa, ON
Canada K1P 5G4
acta.ca

ACTA is a national trade association representing the retail travel sector of Canada's tourism industry.

Institute of Certified Travel Agents (ICTA)
148 Linden St.
Wellesley, MA 02181
icta.com

ICTA is an international, non-profit organisation that educates and certifies travel industry professionals at all career stages.

Books available from ICTA include:

Travel Career Development 7th edition.
Travel Career Development, 7th edition, Student Workbook
Travel Career Development, 7th edition, Instructor's

Resource Manual

Travel Sales and Customer Service, 2nd edition
Travel Sales and Customer Service Instructor's Resource Manual, 2nd edition
Exploring the World: Geography for Travel Professionals

Other Travel Organsations

Airlines Reporting Corporation (ARC)
4100 N. Fairfax Dr., Ste. 600
Arlington, VA 22203-1629
arccorp.com

The purpose of ARC is to be the preferred provider of services related primarily to distribution and settlement of travel purchased in the United States on behalf of ARC's owner airlines, participating carriers, authorised travel agencies and customers.

Amtrak
National Railroad Passenger Corporation
60 Massachusetts Ave. NE, 4th Fl.
Washington, DC 20002-4285
amtrak.com

(For more on railroads, see Chapter 3.)

Cruise Lines International Association
5000 Fifth Ave., Ste. 1407
New York, NY 10110
cruising.org

(For more on cruise lines, see Chapter 3.)

International Airlines Travel Agency Network (IATAN)
300 Garden City Plaza, Ste. 342
Garden City, NY 11530-3302
iatan.org

IATAN provides a vital link between the supplier community and the U.S. travel distribution network.

National Association of Commissioned Travel Agents, Inc. (NACTA)
1101 King St., Ste. 300
Alexandria, VA 22314
nacta.com

NACTA is the travel industry's leading association for independent travel agents, cruise-oriented agents, home-based travel agents, and outside-sales travel agents.

Travel Industry Association (TIA)
1100 New York Ave. NW, Ste. 450
Washington, DC 20005-3934
tia.org

TIA is a non-profit association that represents and speaks for the common interests and concerns of all components of the U.S. travel industry.

United States Tour Operators Association (USTOA)
275 Madison Ave., Ste. 2014
New York, NY 10016
astoa.com

The USTOA is a professional association representing the tour operator industry.

Trade Publications

TravelAge West: travelagewest.com
Travel Agent Magazine: travelagentcentral.com
Travel Tade: traveltrade.com
Travel Weekly: travelweekly.com

6

ROLE OF PUBLIC RELATIONS IN TOURISM

The travel industry must rely heavily on advertising and promotion to attract the crowds of travellers on whom it depends. Advertising, on the scale required to promote a Caribbean island, for example, is very expensive. When funds are scarce for advertising, the ingenious public relations professional fills the void by obtaining publicity through visits by travel writers and travel agents and celebrities, through celebrations and fairs and local events that merit press notice, and through all manner of innovative activities that legitimately draw attentions. Even with a generous advertising budget, all these activities remain important in continuing to attract travellers.

Persuasion through communication is the job of the public relations professional. More specifically, public relations for travel concerns the relations of corporations, governments, hotels, carriers, resorts, cities, and other organisation with their own employees, business travellers, pleasure travellers, and the public at large. Among the media used by public relations experts to influence people are newspapers, magazines, books, radio, television, speeches, photographs, advertisements, surveys, exhibitions, charts, receptions and parties. Workers in public relations may serve inside the organisation being publicised, or they may belong to an outside company specialising in public relations for one or many organisations.

In 2000, public relations managers held approximately 74,000 jobs, according to the Bureau of Labour Statistics. There were approximately 707,000 advertising, marketing, promotions, public relations and sales managers working in all industries in 2000.

History

From the most ancient times rulers paid writers and songsmiths to create works that praised the ruler, inspired patriotism, and persuaded people of the worthiness of the current war.

These were direct, naïve public relations efforts, and there are thousands of similar examples throughout history. But the term *public relations* did not come into use until early in this century. Before that, the Roman Catholic Church had instituted the word *propaganda* to describe its efforts to mold public opinion in the Counter-Reformation, and press agents were employed by both the North and the South in the Civil War to influence European public opinion. *Propaganda* eventually became a dirty work because people realised that much of it was false. Similarly, the term *press agent* is seldom used now because of the press agents in covering up or glorifying nefarious schemes of the robber barons of American industry in the late 1800s. The ridiculously excessive publicity stunts of press agents for Hollywood stars and other celebrities also added to their tainted image.

Public relations in its modern context started largely with Ivy L. Lee and Edward L. Betrays. Lee, hired in 1906 as publicity adviser to the Pennsylvania Railroad, began a policy of openness and frankness with reporters. For example, instead of trying to suppress press awareness of a terrible train wreck, he invited reporters to the scene and helped them to determine and report the cause of the accident.

Rather than just accepting orders to flaunt good news or suppress bad news, Lee and Betrays both gave advice to their clients. Betrays studied the people he was trying to influence and decided there were several different "publics" to be reached, and each had to be approached in the most effective way.

In 1927, John W. Hill, a newspaperman, opened a one-man public relations company in Cleveland. His firm, Hill and Knowlton, became the largest public relations firm in the world, with offices in New York and seven other U.S. cities, as well as in ten European and Asian cities. Mr. Hill, who died in 1977, once said:

> Since the aim of public relations is to inform and convince, the good public relations person has a talent both for understanding and for telling. He enjoys explaining things to others and, like a good debater, wants to persuade. The public relations person thus tends to have an aptitude for expression. He is likely to be a good writer or speaker. Choosing the right word at the right time is of real importance to him, for he is sensitive to people's responses. The good public relations person has curiosity and thoroughness, too. To convince others, he must himself know; and to know, he has to dig. Thus, the good public relations person has factual knowledge, but knows people, too—how and why they react, when and how to present his message. He must be concerned equally with the big problem and the small detail.

David Ogilvy, an advertising genius, emphasised the value of public relations in promoting tourism:

> Give your public relations budget priority over your advertising budget. . . . There is almost no limit to the amount of free publicity a country can get in newspapers, magazines, television and radio provided you don't starve your public relations people. . . . If I were running a national tourism office in the United States, I wouldn't spend a penny on advertising until I had spent $250,000 on public relations.

And as the Public Relations Society points out:

> Public relations, at its best does not only tell an organisation's "story" to its publics. The public relations practitioner also helps shape his organisation and the way it performs.

Job Responsibilities

There can be a great deal of variety in pubic relations work. The functions of the public relations agency or division can be broken down into eight specific kinds of work:

1. Conducting research and evaluation.
2. Defining goals and planning public relations campaigns.
3. Building working relationships.
4. Writing and editing.
5. Disseminating information.
6. Producing communications.

7. Developing special events.
8. Speaking publicly.

Conducting research and evaluation involves gathering the available facts necessary to a firmly based public relations effort, then narrowing the focus to those areas where changes can be effected. Library research, personal conversations, interviews with key people, and broad surveys of public opinion are some of the methods used in this process.

Defining the goals of a public relations campaign avoids waste of effort and money. At this point, plans are made for the amount on money to be spent on each main part of the project and for particular people to be employed to get the message across to selected audiences. For example, a compaign to bring more tourists to Hawaii might entail either sending a troupe of hula dancers and singers to perform at business luncheon meetings in the twenty-five largest American cities, or sending some Hawaiian swimming champions to perform at swimming meets around the country. The cooperation of people outside the public relations office must be obtained will in advance, and they must understand their job as ambassadors with a message.

Building working relationships is essential in public relations. Much of the effectiveness of campaigns depends upon favours given and received, information provided on the basis of personal friendship, and newspaper space or broadcast time made available because an editor or broadcaster likes and trusts a public relations person. Within a company, a public relations worker must sometimes work through the personnel department, the legal department, or the marketing department, and her or his effectiveness is in direct ratio to personal acceptability.

Writing and editing form a major part of public relations work because print is the communications medium most often used. Among the writings public relations people are press releases, brochures, pamphlets, booklets, annual reports, articles for trade magazines, statistics, survey results, technical data, newsletters, shareholder reports, and employee publications, as well as film scripts and speeches to be given by key personnel. Writing that is clear, lively, and effective in putting a message across will be an important part of any public relations work. As a matter of fact, many people who write well and want to be novelists eventually find themselves in public relations, where they are likely to be paid better (and more regularly) than they would be for writing novels.

Disseminating information to the appropriate editors of the relevant print and broadcast media is essential to communicating the messages of public relations to its publics. Keeping open the channels to these editors requires toleration, cooperation, and knowledge of the editors' needs and schedules. People in public relations do their best to be known, liked and trusted by editors.

Producing communications includes all the techniques of art, photography, layout, typography, printing, cinema, television, and other means of putting the message across. Public relations workers must work with specialists in these fields and must know enough about the techniques to see that they are used with utmost effectiveness.

Developing special events may take thousands of forms. A state tourist promotion director may invite a dozen writers on a tour of her or his state in hopes of getting them to write and sell favourable articles. A state such as Virginia may host a party for several hundred writers and editors in New York and show a promotional film to increase their interest in Virginia. An essay contest on local history may be held for high school students in order to obtain newspaper publicity for local historical shrines when the winners are awarded their prizes. News conferences, travel shows, ski shows, boat shows, camping shows, canoe races, and many kinds of demonstrations of equipment also are used to promote travel. Public relations people may do the original planning for these events and then obtain the cooperation of the principals who speak, compete, or otherwise earn the interest of the public. Finally, the public relations people prepare news stories and reports about the event, easing the way for reporters to write their own stories.

Speaking in public is often important in public relations work. Many times a politician, company president or celebrity, whose presence makes an event newsworthy, delivers a speech written by a public relations worker. A public relations worker needs to be an adept public speaker because he or she may often be asked to represent the client, company, or government by speaking at various types of meetings.

Public relations work is often frantic. If riots in a city cause prospective visitors to cancel reservations in the whole region, public relations workers must spread the word that all areas are not affected. An earthquake, a hurricane, a political coup, or an outbreak of disease can cause similar reactions and must be countered by public relations efforts. Such crises may involve work, travel during personal time to the site of the difficulty, and statements from authorities to be quoted to the press. An airplane crash always gets headlines and inevitably causes a drop in bookings on the airline. Public relations people for the carrier have to work around the clock for weeks after a crash, trying to restore the reputation of the carrier in the minds of the travelling public.

Ideally a public relations programme is based on solid research, evaluation of facts, and determination of goals and schedules. Its various steps are planned for a period of a year to several years in advance.

Consider, for example, an island in the Caribbean or Mediterranean, for which a U.S. public relations agency is engaged to promote tourism. The island has only one hotel, small and very luxurious, but it has an ambitious construction programme. In the first year, the agency might arrange visits by a number of celebrities to the one hotel, to build it up in the public mind as a "jet-set hideaway". As the island constructed the necessary infrastructure for development (water, sewage and utility systems), the agency would report these items in the professional travel press, so travel agents would be reminded constantly of a new mass market to come. As new hotels were completed, the agency and the hotels would cooperate in holding highly publicised opening parties and celebrations, and shortly thereafter they would bring hundreds of travel agents on free or low-cost familiarisation tours. Then package deals with airlines, hotels, and other services might be developed and publicised. Meanwhile, articles about the island's food would be sent to food editors; articles on crafts, history, sports, architecture, native habits, shows, and anything of news interest would go to other appropriate editors. The volume of news releases that can keep flooding out continually about even a little island is staggering.

This volume of press releases causes another problem. Every day, travel editors on metropolitan newspapers receive one or two mailbags full of publicity material. They cannot possibly print more than 1 per cent of it, so the public relations writer has to use a lot of ingenuity to make releases and pictures distinctive enough to persuade an editor to even look at them.

Education and Training

The young person aiming toward a professional carrier in public relations should consider graduation from college essential. Many of today's top people in the field arrived by way of journalism, and they consider a degree in journalism, plus a year or two of experience on a newspaper, the best preparation for the field. However, specific education for public relations has been expanding rapidly. Many colleges and universities offered at least one course in public relations, and more than two hundred colleges had degree programmes or special curricula in which public relations was an important part of a student's course of study. In addition, there are more than 220 chapters of the Public Relations Student Society of America on campuses nationwide.

Journalism or mass communications schools or departments administer most public relations programmes. The Accrediting Council on Education in Journalism and Mass Communications (the ACEJMC) is the only agency authorised to accredit such schools or departments. Collegiate public relations curricula may be found in schools of journalism, communications, education, or business administration. Programmes leading to a doctorate or a master's degree in public relations are now offered in more than sixty institutions.

In addition, an accreditation programme—The Universal Accreditation Programme—was formed in January 1998. The purpose of accreditation is to unify and advance the profession by identifying those who have demonstrated broad knowledge, experience, and professional judgment in the field. The programme seeks to improve public relations practice. The designation Accredited in Public Relations (APR) signifies a high professional level of experience and competence.

Earnings and Job Outlook

According to a Public Relations Society of America study, salaries in public relations fall into a very broad range. The median range for public relations personnel is $53,000 a $4,000 increase from 1995. In 1999, salaries ranged from $28,000 to $147,000.

The job prospects outlook for public relations workers is favourable because the industry keeps growing as businesses add public relations departments independent agencies expand their activities. According to the Bureau of Labour Statistics, jobs for public relations specialists are expected to increase by 36.1 per cent between 2000 and 2010.

Sources of Information

Brochures on careers in public relations are available from the following organisations:

The Accrediting Council on Education in Journalism and Mass Communications (ACEJMC)
Stauffer-Flint Hall
1435 Jayhawk Blvd.
Lawrence, KS 66045-7575
ku.edu/~acejmc/index.html

ACEJMC is the agency that is responsible for the evaluation of professional journalism and mass communications programmes in colleges and universities.

Canadian Public Relations Society, Inc. (CPRS)
One Yonge St., Ste. 1801
Toronto, ON
Canada M5E 1W7
cprstoronto.com

The CPRS represents more than eighteen hundred public relations and communications professionals in Canada.

PR and Marketing Network
1201 Sevan Loks Rd. Ste. 300
Potomac, MD 20854
prandmarketing.com

PR and Marketing Network holds PR and marketing seminars, published newsletters and E-letters, holds award programmers and does custom publishing.

Public Relations Society of America
33 Irving Pl.
New York, NY 10003
prsa.org

Public Relations Student Society of America
33 Irving Pl.
New York, NY 10003
prssa.org

The declared purpose of PRSSA is to cultivate a favourable and mutually advantageous relationship between students and professional public relations practitioners.

Travel Industry Association (TIA)
1100 New York Ave. NW, Ste. 450
Washington, DC 20005-3934
tia.org

TIA is a non-profit association that represents and speaks for the common interests and concerns of all components of the U.S. travel industry. It publishes *Travel Industry Public Relations Handbook,* an easy to read, step-by-step "how to" guide to eight important areas of travel and tourism public relations written by travel and tourism public relations professionals in the field.

7

RECREATION AND AMUSEMENT

Some of the fastest-growing jobs in the tourism industry are in the recreation and amusement field. In 2000 there were more than 1.7 million people working for approximately 102,000 establishments classified in the amusement and recreation fields. A large percentage of these jobs are directly related to travel and tourism. Basically, and activity that occupies a traveller's time is part of the amusement and recreation fields in the travel and tourism industry. These would include employment relating to fitness, boating, hunting, fishing, white-water adventures, amusement parks, museums, gaming and in the entertainment industries such as theater or musical events.

Fitness has been a prime concern of North Americans and Europeans since the early 1980s. Hotels around the world now have running tracks and health clubs as standard facilities. Tennis, skiing, and other active sports attract more and more people. Golf vacations continue to rise. The Travel Industry Association (TIA) found that one in eight U.S. travellers played golf on a one-way trip of at least on hundred miles in 2000. Special interest travel such as adventure travel including off-road biking, mountain climbing; scuba diving, bird-watching, sailing, or canoeing is fashionable. Increasing leisure time has led to the proliferation of resorts and sports areas and the growth of the National Park System, a well as state and local parks. In 2000 the number of visitors to state parks broke records: 766 million visits occurred in the 4,710 areas operated by America's state park agencies. Overnight stays in parks, campgrounds, group lodges, resort facilities and marinas were recorded in 1999 at 61.8 million. The consequence of the proliferation of these types of travel vacations has increased the demand for recreation leaders and administrators. In 1972 there were 55,000 recreation workers in year-round jobs; by 2000 recreation and fitness workers held about 427,000 jobs and many additional workers held summer jobs in this occupation. In 2000 about 63 per cent of those employed in this field were recreation workers; the rest were fitness trainers and aerobics instructors. Of those with year-round jobs as recreation workers, more than one-third worked in park and recreation departments of municipal and county governments. The Canadian Parks/Recreation Association stated in 1984: "Recreation stands out as a career with a stable future."

Public and private support of recreation, although expanding rapidly now, is far from new. The stadium in ancient Greece, the amphitheater in Rome, public gardens, parks, zoos, swimming pools, baths, playgrounds, gymnasiums, opera houses, theaters, dance halls, athletic fields—all attest to people's inveterate devotion to recreation.

Since World War II, the number of hours in the average worker's week has been reduced, vacations have become longer, more holidays have been observed, and the moving of holidays to Mondays of Fridays to lengthen the weekends has increased holiday travel.

In 1978 the U.S. National Park Service more than doubled the amount of land under its jurisdiction, to over 87 million acres in 384 parks. Many states also have set aside more land for parks, and commercial campgrounds and Recreational Vehicle (RV) parks have sprung up around many national and state parks to accommodate constantly overflowing crowds of campers. The National Association of RV Parks and Campgrounds states that in 1999, there were more than seventy-five million camper nights occupying one million RV sites. The industry's total revenue was just under $6 billion. Trends include increase in Internet usage at RV sites, water amenities at campgrounds, the attraction of non-campers and minority campers in the Northeast and Southwest, and a growing number of single females and single parents attracted to the social settings of campgrounds. In addition, employment at parks and campgrounds is shifting from teen and college students to older retirees looking for a more nomadic lifestyle.

As a consequence of this growth, completely new industries have been established to manufacture recreation vehicles, houseboats, camping gear, snow skis and water skis, hang gliders and dozens of other kinds of recreation equipment. New recreational villages have sprung up—second-home and time-share condominium communities adjacent to ski areas, beaches, golf courses, tennis compounds and primitive forests. All of these developments explain why the need for recreation workers in expanding so rapidly.

Job Responsibilities

The job responsibilities of those working in the recreation and amusement industries are outlined below:

Recreation

What specific jobs do recreation workers perform? They teach dancing and lead social get-togethers to help people meet each other at resorts. They lead calisthenic sessions on beaches and in gymnasiums, aiding people in keeping fit or losing weight. They serve as lifeguards; swimming, tennis, and golf instructors; and coaches for all sorts of athletic teams. They also lead singing groups and impromptu bands and orchestras, and they enlist acting talent and put on plays or musical dramas at resorts.

Some recreation workers concentrate on activities with certain age groups; for instance, teaching skiing to children ages three years and up, or keeping senior citizens busy with checkers and other sedentary activities. Many recreation workers teach handcrafts such as leatherwork, beadwork, basket weaving macramé, batik, sewing, crocheting and model building.

Recreation workers can be divided into three major groups according to their responsibilities. In the first group, made up of camp counsellors and recreation leaders, the work consists of teaching people to do things they can enjoy in their leisure time and leading them in sports and games.

The second group consists of specialists in particular activities. In a large comp for young people, one specialist might spend all of her or his time teaching people how to make things out of leather, holding several classes each day. Another such specialist is the golf professional at a resort or country club. Recreation workers who have enough experience and enough capital sometimes start their own businesses such as camps, hobby shops, outfitters, trail-guide services, boat-rental services, white-water rafting services and craft instruction schools.

Above these two groups are members of the third group, the supervisors and administrators of recreation programmes, summer camps, shipboard passenger activity programmes; and the directors of city parks and recreation departments and of leisure programmes for non-profit organisations, corporations, institutions, and the armed services.

Recreation administration involves major responsibility for planning and administering recreation and park programmes to meet the needs and interests of the area served. Responsibilities include budgeting, trend forecasting, marketing, and other promotional techniques to attract participants to their recreation programmes. Job titles include director of recreation and parks, recreation supervisor, recreation center director, recreation leader, recreation worker and park planner.

In natural resource and park management, responsibilities are as diverse a wildlife management, park management, soil conser vation, watershed management, and forestry. Job titles include park ranger, park police, park manager, or wildlife manager.

Today there are more than twelve thousand days and resident camps of varying types and lengths. Each summer more than ten million children and adults take advantage of these organised recreational and educational opportunities. Camp management requires skill, vision and innovative strategies to be successful. Camps vary by style and format to meet many interests. Outdoor activities of hiking, swimming, sports and games, arts and crafts, and nature awareness are offered; some have special emphasis on programmes such as horseback riding, water sports, music, or adventure challenge activities. Summer camps employ more than one million adults to work as counsellors, programme/activity leaders, unit and programme directors/supervisors, and in support services roles such as maintenance, administration, food service and health care.

The American Gaming Association (AGA) reports that in 2001 there were more than 434 commercial casinos operating in eleven states, directly employing more than 364,484 people with revenues of $25.6 billion. AGA also reports that 30 per cent of U.S. households gamble at a casino, making an average of 5.4 trips during the year. In addition, during the past decade, the casino workforce has increased more than 79 per cent, with the creation of seventeen thousand new jobs in the commercial casino industry. Jobs range from blackjack or poker dealer to behind-the-scenes jobs as pit clerk, cage cashier, slot technician, or surveillance officer.

Amusement Parks

Amusement parks in North America had sunk to a low ebb—notorious for their filthy food and atmosphere, pickpockets, confidence men, and dangerous, unsafe rides—when Walt Disney launched Disneyland in California in 1955. Disneyland revolutionised the industry. Everything was kept spic and span; blooming flowers and shrubs were everywhere. Most of the personnel in contact with the public were wholesome high school and college students who were friendly and helpful. Engineering ingenuity was put to work to design new rides and other excitements and to improve old ones. All uniforms were clean, neat and colourful. Something of particular interest was offered for all ages.

Large theme parks and water parks can now be found in every state in the United States. Many of these parks have hotels in or adjacent to them, making it convenient for families. It is estimated that a total of 450 parks in North America generated total attendance of more than 317 million in 2000 and produced an economic impact of $9.6 billion. The U.S. theme park revenue will continue to grow, estimated by Pricewaterhouse Coopers at 5.1 per cent through 2005. An interesting fact is that over the next ten years, the U.S. population age forty-five and over will grow considerably. This age group does not traditionally have a burning desire to visit a traditional theme park. Park operators, looking for new markets and revenue, are finding ways to target this market—made up primarily of adult couples without children—with adult-oriented rides and golf courses, upscale hotels, restaurants, spas and nighttime entertainment.

Employment at amusement parks is a two-tier affair. There is a small cadre of permanent staff and a huge horde of part-timers—more than two hundred thousand in North America during the summer. The permanent crew includes executives in charge of maintenance, operations, sales, purchasing, advertising, public relations, food and rides and their small full-time staffs. Descriptions for permanent jobs vary. They can range from project scheduler, whose responsibilities include "the development, implementation and maintenance of plans and schedules for attraction projects from conception through completion"; to general manager of a $7 million start-up leisure attraction; to park operations manager, who is responsible for "the management of multiple amusement parks and entertainment facilities."

A few parks in warm areas are open all year, but most, influenced by climate and school vacations, operate only in summer and on spring and fall weekends. All have cyclical busy and slow seasons.

Requirements

In such a broad industry as recreation and amusement, requirements for the many types of jobs naturally vary from job to job band and from employer to employer. Employment conditions for recreation workers are usually very pleasant; they are helping people to enjoy life and to learn simple skills that give a feeling of accomplishment. Generally a recreation worker should be an outgoing, gregarious person who is interested in other people and eager to help and to teach. The work should bring pleasure to the recreation professional, because he or she must work when most other people are at leisure—evenings, weekends and the summer vacation months.

Education and Training

More than 40 per cent of workers in the recreation and amusement industries have no formal education past high school. The services jobs are traditionally filled by young, unskilled workers the majority of time during seasonal months.

To obtain a year-round position in recreation, considerable experience is highly desirable, as is graduation from at least a two-year—or preferably, a four-year—college. Varying degrees of certification are required depending on the job and employer. In a physical fitness facility, a fitness trainer or aerobics instructor may require a specific type of certification by the facility owner. For a full-time position as a recreation administrator, applicants are usually college graduates with a major in parks, recreation, or leisure services. Persons with academic preparation in parks, recreation, or leisure studies; physical education; fitness management; and related fields generally have better prospects for carrer advancement. The profession of directing recreation is a young one that is growing rapidly; as it grows, educational requirements will become more stringent. A person with foresight and determination will complete four years of college and go on to obtain a master's degree, and perhaps even a doctorate, to avoid being prevented from advancing later because of a lack of formal educational credentials.

Many recreation workers specialising in music, drama and art have graduate degrees. Graduate work might well include courses such as business administration, since programme directors must prepare budgets, allocate funds, and conduct their recreation programmes in a businesslike fashion. Other graduate courses should concentrate mainly on the recreation professional's specific area of interest.

Camp directors are required to have some know-how and background in technical fields such a nutrition, food service, facility design and maintenance, risk management, marketing, and personnel and business management. This job also necessitates the blending of the principles of social group work, recreation, child development, physical education, health and wellness, psychology and education.

In the amusement park industry, for temporary or seasonal workers, the parks tend to look for youth, wholesomeness, and an outgoing personality. Education is helpful but not important. For permanent positions, however, knowledge counts—a degree in business administration, public relations, advertising, restaurant management, or food service (or perhaps hotel and restaurant management if the park owns a hotel) is an advantage. If you want a career in amusement parks, go after a college degree, and gain valuable experience during your time off by working in several departments of various parks.

Earnings and Job Outlook

Earnings in the recreation and amusement industries are generally low, reflecting the large numbers of part-time and seasonal jobs. Non-supervisory workers in these services positions average $262 a week in 2000, compared with $474 in the private industry. Median hourly earnings of fitness trainers and aerobics instructors in all industries in 2000 were $10.96, and the top 10 per cent earned $25.98 or more. In 2000, earnings of these workers in the miscellaneous amusement and recreation services industry, which includes commercial fitness clubs, were $12.22 an hour; fitness trainers and aerobics instructors in civic and social associations earned $ 9.03. Earnings for successful self-employed personal trainers can be much higher. Median hourly earnings of amusement and recreation attendants in the recreation and amusement industry in 2000 were $6.63. Benefits in amusement and theme parks include free passes to the park, transportation to and from work, housing, discounts on park merchandise and even sometimes scholarships.

According to the Bureau of Labour Statistics, jobs for recreation and amusement services workers are expected to increase by approximately 35 per cent between 2000 and 2010. These jobs are ranked as one of the highest-growth occupations in this ten-year period. Increasing income, leisure time, and the recognition of the health benefits of being fit contribute to this high-growth services industry. An increase in the average age of the U.S. population will lead to an increase in markets that cater to an elderly clientele, such as golf courses or cruise ships.

Sources of Information

American Alliance for Health, Physical Education, Recreation and Dance (AAHPERD)

1900 Association Dr.
Reston, VA 22091
aahperd.org

AAHPERD is the largest organisation of professionals supporting and assisting those involved in physical education, leisure, fitness, dance, health promotion and education.

American Camping Association (ACA)
Bradford Woods
5000 State Road 67N
Martinsville, IN 46151
acacamps.org

The ACA is a community of more than six thousand camping professionals.

American Gaming Association (AGA)
555 Thirteenth St. NW, Ste. 1010 East
Washington DC 20004
americangaming.org.

The AGA represents the commercial casino entertainment industry.

Canadian Association for Health, Physical Education, Recreations, and Dance (CAHPERD)
403-2197 Riverside Dr.
Ottawa, ON
Canada K1H 7X3
cahperd.ca

CAHPERD is a national, charitable, voluntary-sector organisation whose primary concern is to influence the healthy development of children and youth by advocating for quality, school-based physical and health education.

Canadian Parks/Recreation Association
404-2197 Riverside Dr.
Ottawa, ON
Canada K1H 7X3
cpra.ca

CPRA is a national voice for the Canadian parks and recreation industry.

International Association of Amusement Parks and Attractions (IAAPA)
1448 Duke St.
Alexandria, VA 22314
iaapa.org

IAAPA exists to foster the highest degree of professionalism within the amusement industry, to promote the market for its goods and services, to gather and disseminate information on the industry, and to represent the interests of the industry before government.

National Amusement Park Historical Association (NAPHA)
P.O. Box 83
Mt. Prospect, IL 60056

NAPHA is an international organisation dedicated to the preservation and enjoyment of the amusement and theme park industry—past, present and future.

National Association of RV Parks and Campgrounds (ARVC)
113 Park Ave.
Falls Church, VA 22046
arvc.org

ARVC is the trade association representing the commercial RV park and campground industry throughout the United States.

National Recreation and Park Association (NRPA)
22377 Belomont Ridge Rd.
Ashburn, VA 20148
nrpa.org

NRPA's goal is to promote public awareness and support for recreation, park and leisure services.

Parks Canada
25 Eddy St.
Hull, Quebec
Canada K1A0M5
http://parkscanada.pch.gc.ca

Parks Canada's mandate is to protect and present nationally significant examples of Canada's natural and cultural heritage and to foster public understanding, appreciation and enjoyment in ways that ensure their ecological and commemorative integrity for present and future generations.

8

TRAVEL WRITING FOR MONEY

In English slang a few generations ago, a "traveller's tale" meant a tall story—a highly coloured and exaggerated account of adventures in exotic and faraway lands. Most of the world's literatures have included such reports. Homer's *Odyssey,* dating from about 850 B.C., not only relates the adventures of Odysseus (Ulysses) over the twenty years it took him to come home from the Trojan War, but also describes accurately many parts of the Mediterranean world that he visited.

One of the world's most fascinating travel classics is *The Book of Marco Polo.* Fortunately for the world, this Venetian man of action, after his epochal journeys across Asia and his twenty-four years in the service of Kublai Khan, was taken prisoner in a war between Venice and Genoa. Using his carefully written travel notebooks, in 1298 he dictated to a fellow captive, the scribe Rustigielo of Pisa, the book that disclosed Cathay to Europe. Christopher Columbus had a copy of this bock and made notations on more than seventy pages. His object, when he sailed in 1492, was to reach Marco Polo's Cathay.

Another monumental travel writer was Richard Hakluyt of England, who became archdeacon of Westminster and is buried in Westminster Abbey. Between 1582 and 1600 he wrote several books, chief of which is his *Principal Navigations, Voyages, and Discoveries of the English Nation,* which describes all the great sea expeditions of English captains to America, the Arctic, the Pacific, and around the world.

If only some chronicler had joined the fishing expeditions of early Portuguese, French, English and Scandinavian fishermen, we might know much more about ancient landings in North America. It is suspected that there was fishing from European ships on the Grand Banks off Newfoundland and Nova Scotia as far back as a thousand years ago.

The first important analysis of the United States and its life is *De la democratie en Amerique (Democracy in America),* published in 1835 by Comte Alexis de Tocqueville. Sent to examine the U.S. penitentiary system for the French Government, de Tocqueville wrote his report on prisons, and then, in *Democracy in America,* he described American life with such penetration as had never been applied before, and seldom since. He perceived that the great difference between Eurpoe and America was the American insistence on equality and he showed how this affected every facet of life, from emergent literature to science, religion, philosophy, the arts, language, business, the family, the military and manners. He didn't care much for our ancestors' manners, but he foresaw that the influence of democracy would bring about the emancipation of women.

De Tocqueville's work would not be considered travel writing by some persons—those who believe that travel writing concerns itself solely with the traveller's transportation, accommodations, shopping and recreation. But, in reality, this is the very best kind of travel writing, because de Tocqueville delivers that most precious gift—insight.

The insight of the travel writer can bring the reader to feel kinship with people of another land and another race by showing the universal emotions and motivations behind customs that seem strange, even bizarre. An alert travel writer is always attuned to the subtle emanations of a new place and its people. Every bit of feeling that a place arouses in a travel writer must be savored, perhaps analysed, but certainly fully realised, so that the writer can express it in a way that makes the reader feel it as well.

Two men who strongly influenced the development of travel guidebooks as we know them today were John Murray of London and Karl Baedeker of Koblenz, Germany. John Murray (1808–1892) was the third of a distinguished line of publishers, all bearing the same name. He wrote a series of travel handbooks on the Netherlands, Belgium, France, the Rhine, South Germany and Switzerland.

Karl Baedeker (1801–1859) started a printing plant in Koblenz in 1827. Under an arrangement with John Murray, he published a pocket-sized guidebook on the Rhine, Belgium and the Netherlands in 1839. He subsequently brought out guides covering most of Europe and parts of North America and Asia. These books were so reliable and thorough that the name *Baedeker* became a synonym for the word "guidebook". The era of exaggerated "traveller's tales" had ended. Baedeker started the practice of marking with one or more stars in his books places of special interest or attraction, so travellers with little time could determine quickly what to see. "Starred in *Baedeker*" soon came to mean "well worth seeing". These *Baededer* guides were published from the beginning in German, French and English, and this helped them to gain extemely wide readership.

Modern Travel Guidebooks

In our own time, the mantle of Baedeker graced the shoulders of Eugene Fodor, a native Hungarian who became an American citizen. He was editing travel books by 1936 and began publishing *Fodor's* guides in Paris after World War II. He moved his headquarters to the United States in the 1960s and retired in the late 1970s. For each *Fodor's* guide, authorship is generally shared by a number of writers and researchers—whenever possible, experts residing in the country described by the book. Fodor has died, but his guides live on.

Quite different are the highly personal guidebooks exemplified by Myra Waldo's *Travel and Motoring Guide to Europe* and *Fielding's Travel Guide to Europe* (by Temple Fielding). These popular guidebooks, revised annually, depend for their attraction on the readers' confidence that they can rely upon the taste and preferences of Myra Waldo and the late Temple Fielding.

Arthur Frommer, after travelling through Europe with his wife as inexpensively as possible, wrote *Europe on $5 a Day,* an inexpensive paperback book. The title's assertion that travel could be very inexpensive doubtless inspired many Americans to visit Europe. For millions of young people, it was a bible of essential information, carried around Europe until it was dog-eared and tattered. It was such a success that Frommer started a publishing house, which now keeps a number of authors busy writing and updating more than fifty titles. A single writer or a team of two writers writes each book. Having achieved fame as a travel writer, then as a travel-book publisher, Frommer went on to become a package-tour operator and hotel impresario.

For many readers, escapist literature offers excitement and exotic scenes that take them out of their daily routines. Travel books do this with descriptions of true adventure in jungle exploration or mountain climbing, treasure hunting or visiting natives of lost civilisations, archaeological exploration or sailing traps across an ocean on a raft. This kind of escapist non-fiction permits armchair travel and is at the opposite end of the spectrum of travel writing from the step-by-step *Beadeker.*

In between these opposites are many kinds of books on outdoor life, hunting and fishing, camping, ecology, folklore, local crafts, transportation, skiing, boating, history, cruising, flying, gliding, and so forth. Some of these are written to amaze or amuse the reader, others to give the reader practical advice and instruction.

As travel has become more widespread, the amount of travel coverage in magazines and newspapers has increased. Travel is a major interest, and people do more travelling every year. Another reason for the increase in the number of travel articles is that travel advertising has been increasing from year to year. A magazine or newspaper carrying a great deal of travel advertising must carry a commensurate amount of travel writing; otherwise, readers do not look at the advertising. If a Sunday newspaper's travel section had only advertisements, most people would discard it unread.

Freelance Travel Writing

Making a living as a freelance travel writer is becoming increasingly difficult. Newspapers, whose Sunday travel sections had been the largest market for travel articles, are becoming fewer. As newspapers decline in number, however, all kinds of specialised magazines spring up. They do not use as many travel articles as the newspapers had, and their standards are often higher, but magazines of many kinds use travel articles in hopes of attracting travel advertising. This has increased the number of jobs for staff writers and editors.

A growing thereat to freelance travel writers is the decision by a few of the most prestigious magazines to refuse articles generated by sponsored trips, as a few top newspapers did in the early 1970s.

Although travel writing is important to readers, and therefore essential to magazines and newspapers, it is not a lucrative field for the writers. The reason is an ancient economic one—the law of supply and demand. So many people are willing to write articles on travel for little or nothing, and public relations people supply so many free articles and pictures, that an editor on a slim budget may decide to buy no articles at all, relying solely on free material.

During the economic slowdown of the mid-1970s, when newspapers suffered a shortage of newsprint (paper) and greatly increased costs (ink and labour), many newspapers that had been regular buyers of travel articles from freelancers completely stopped buying. They had their travel editors write articles, they used free articles from public relations sources, and they used articles provided by the wire services at very low cost. This is happening again, as many publications fold due to the economic slowdown.

The Society of American Travel Writers (SATW) was founded in 1956. SATW has approximately 1,460 members and its primary goals are first, to promote responsible journalism; second, to provide professional support and development for its members; and third, to encourage the conservation and preservation of travel resources worldwide. Throughout the years, SATW members have seen changes in the travel writing profession.

Adele Malott, current SATW president, says of the changes:

> Indeed, travel writing has changed in the last decade or so and wi continue to change alongwith the world itself. With the extended us

> of new technology such as computers and the Internet, a travel writer has worldwide research available on his or her desktop and can reach far afield to find new markets for material created. The challenge is being able to keep up with all the new developments and learn to use them. I have always believed that a writer who sells well is one with a specialty and I think that will continue to be the case. Writers who know the psychographics of a travel entity—the student, the family, the senior, the doctor, the professor—will always be able to find a market for their work, primarily because they can provide information beyond the norm.

In 1980 a second national travel writers' organisation was formed—the Travel Journalists Guild (TJG). Composed solely of freelance travel writers and travel photographers, its establishment was necessitated by the fact that freelance objectives could not be pursued in the SATW because they conflicted with the policies that travel editors in SATW had to enforce for their publishers. The founding president of TJG, Bern Keating, performed a signal service for all American freelance writers by obtaining the introduction in the Senate of a bill to amend the copyright law so that publishers would not be permitted to buy other than first serial rights of articles, unless other rights were paid for. The bill had a hearing but did not reach the Senate floor. Many other writers', photographers' and artists' groups joined ranks in support of the amendment, and the fight goes on. Membership is kept small and highly professional.

Travel writing, for most freelance writers, does not earn enough to cover the costs of the necessary travel. Recognising this (and hoping to obtain coverage of their attractions or facilities) airlines, resorts, hotels, railroads, cruise lines, and local and national governments often invite travel writers on press trips and cover part or all of their expenses.

In the early 1970s, several prestigious newspapers declared they would no longer buy travel articles based on "sponsored" trips. One editor went so far as to say this was a dishonest way of obtaining information for an article, despite the fact that his publication pays quite low rates, demands "magazine quality" articles, and pays no expenses. Under these conditions, of course, a travel writer specialising in faraway places must have other income in order to write for these papers. This cuts out the professional freelancer, and in fact, leaves this article market to those who do not depend on travel writing for their income–business travellers, pleasure travellers with a flair for writing and others for whom travel writing is a sideline.

The same newspapers that reject press trips as unethical accept free tickets to plays, ballets, concerts and sports events for their theater critics, dance critics music critics, and sportswriters. They also pay the expenses of any reporter who must travel to cover a story.

Another difficulty for people trying to become full-time professional freelance travel writers is that the "star' system is in effect at most of the best magzines. An editor wants to publish as many articles by celebrities as possible, so their names can be printed on the cover to help sell the magazine. This makes it difficult for a newcomer to break into the field and to sell enough articles to keep going.

This look at the problems shows that freelance travel writing is, in general, an insecure field. For those with talent and persistence, however, it is a fascinating way to earn a living.

Travel Editors

A position as travel editor of a magazine or newspaper is much more secure than that of a freelancer. There is a regular salary, there are regular hours in the publication's offices, and, in the case of most metropolitan newspapers, there is a union contract to regulate working conditions. The Newspaper Guild, the union for reporters and editors, has been quite militant about obtaining good salaries and other benefits for its members.

Travel writing and travel editing are generally not recognised as specialties open to beginning reporters and editors in the newspaper world, so the neophyte must begin as a general reporter or copy editor. As more educational institutions develop curricula in Transportation, Travel and Tourism (TTT); Hospitality and Tourism Management; or Hospitality, Restaurant, and Institutional Management, newspapers may begin to place these graduates in assignments that cover these subjects.

There are so few magazine travel editors that it is difficult to generalise about them, but it can be said that a college education is required for such work. Some travel editors are journalism graduates, but many are graduates in fine arts. For both newspapers and magazines, the master's degree is becoming increasingly necessary.

The work of a travel editor varies greatly from one publication to another. On some newspapers and magazines, the travel editor is actually the sole travel writer. Richard Joseph, for example, was travel editor of *Esquire* from 1946 until he died while on a trip in the late 1970s. He generally wrote two articles for each issue, and *Esquire* seldom bought any other travel articles.

To become any kind of a travel writer, editor, or broadcaster today, an undergraduate college education is essential, and graduate degrees help. A travel photographer does not need college training but must have a great deal of technical expertise, as well as flair for the work. The competition in this work is very stiff—a magazine editor selecting photographs to illustrate an article often will have one to two hundred or more offered, of which only one to five may be used.

Sources of Information

American Society of Journalists and Authors (ASJA)
1501 Broadway, Ste. 302
New York, NY 10036
asja.org/index9.php

ASJA is the nation's leading organisation of independent non-fiction writers.

Association of Women in Communications (AWAC)
(formerly Women in Communications)
780 Ritchie Hwy., Ste. 28-S
Severna Park, MD 21146
womcom.org/indexie.html

AWAC is a professional organisation that champions the advancement of women across all communications disciplines by recognising excellence, promoting leadership, and positioning its members at the fore-front of the evolving communications era.

Canadian Newspaper Association (CAN)
321 Bloor St., East
Toronto, ON
Canada M4W 1E7
cna-acj.ca/default.asp?language=english

CNA is a non-profit organisation, representing one hundred Canadian daily newspapers (English and French).

The Dow Jones Newspaper Fund, Inc. (DJNF)
P.O. Box 300
Princeton, NJ 08540
http://djnewspaperfund.dowjones.com/fund

DJNF is a non-profit foundation supported by the Dow Jones Foundation and provides internships and scholarships to college students, career literature, fellowships for high school journalism teachers and publications' advisers, and training for college journalism instructors.

East West News Bureau (EWNB) and the North American Travel Journalists Association (NATJA)
531 Main St., #902
El Segundo, CA 90245

EWNB/NATJA is a professional association dedicated to the travel, food, wine and hospitality industries. EWNB's goals are to support high-quality professional journalism, to promote travel and leisure activities to the public, to encourage international collaboration among its industries, and to honor the excellence of journalists throughout the world.

The Newspaper Guild (TNG)
8611 Second Ave.
Silver Spring, MD 20910
newsguild.org

The TNG is a media union. Wage scale information is found on its website.

Periodical Writers Association of Canada (PWAC)
54 Wolseley St.
Toronto, ON
Canada M5T 1A5
web.net/~pwac

The PWAC mandate is to protect and promote the rights and careers of independent, freelance periodical writers.

Society of American Travel Writers (SATW)
1500 Sunday Dr., Ste. 102
Raleigh, NC 27607
satw.org

SATW is a tax-exempt professional association whose purpose is to promote responsible journalism, provide professional support and development for its members, and encourage the conservation and preservation of travel resources worldwide.

Travel Journalists Guild (TJG)
P.O. Box 10643
Chicago, IL 60610
tjgonline.com

TJG is a select group of freelance writers, photographers, film-makers, and artists who specialise in travel worldwide.

9

TOURISM: INCOME AND EMPLOYMENT

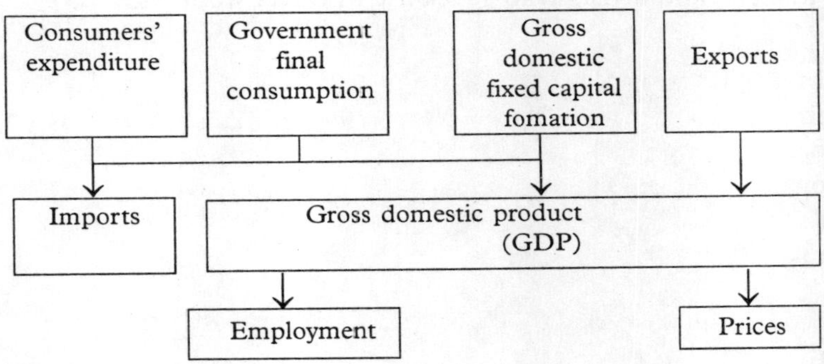

Objectives

The aim of this chapter is to examine the other side of this question, and ask how the leisure and tourism sector contributes to the general level of economic activity. In particular it will examine the contribution of leisure and tourism to national output, national income and national expenditure, to the level of employment and consider the question of inflation.

By studying this chapter students should be able to:

- distinguish between microeconomics and macroeconomics;
- measure the total level of economic activity in an economy;
- distinguish between changes in real and money GNP;
- measure the contribution of leisure and tourism to GNP;

- understand the contribution of leisure and tourism to employment;
- utilise simple economic models of the macroeconomy;
- understand and apply the multiplier principle;
- measure inflation in the leisure and tourism sector;
- interpret government policy in this area.

GNP and the Level of Leisure and Tourism Activity

Macroeconomics

Microeconomic issues concerning the actions of individuals (demand) and firms (supply) and their interaction to determine prices in specific markets (e.g. the market for television sets, the market for air travel).

Macroeconomic are issues that affect the whole economy. Macroeconomics deals with aggregates. Thus, it adds together the spending of individuals to calculate consumers' expenditure, or aggregate demand. It adds together the output of individual organisations to measure national output or product. Similarly, the general price level and rate of inflation are investigated rather than prices in individual markets.

A Simple Macroeconomic Model

Figure 9.1 illustrates a simple model of the national economy.

The economy is divided into two sectors, households and firms. Households own factors of production whilst firms utilise factors of production to produce goods and services. It is assumed in this initial model that all the output of firms is sold, and all income is spent. Additionally, there is no government activity, no savings or investment, and no international trade.

These are two flows in this system. First, 'real' flows are designated by unbroken lines. These represent the flow of factors of production (land, labour and capital) from households to firms, and the flow of goods and services, made from these factors of production, from firms to households. Second, 'money' flows are designated by broken lines. These represent factor rewards and payments for goods and services. For example, if a member of a household works for a firm it supplies the factor of labour and receives the reward of wages in

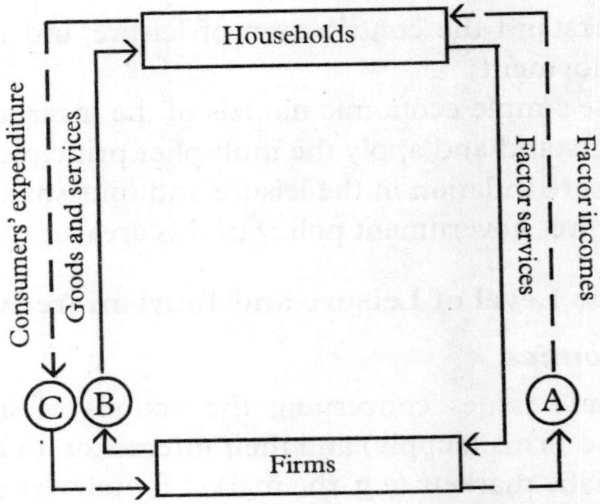

Fig. 9.1 The circular flow of income.

payment. This payment can then be used to purchase goods and services from firms.

In this simple model of the economy firms buy factors of production to make goods and services, and households sell factors of production to buy goods and services. The model can be used to illustrate the concept of national income. National income is a measure of the total level of economic activity which takes place in an economy over a year. In Figure 9.1, if the total flow of money at point A was measured over a year, this would represent the level of national income. The same picture can be viewed from different angles. The total value of goods and services passing point B over a year would represent national output or national product, and the total amount of expenditure passing point C over a year would represent national expenditure. This gives an important accounting identity.

National income = national product = national expenditure

GNP and its Measurement

The key rule in deciding how an item should be treated for national income calculation is whether it represents income earned by or output (or expenditure on that output) produced by, UK factors of production. The three methods of measuring GDP are described in outline below.

Income Method

In this method incomes are added up. Stock appreciation (the increase in the value of firms' stocks due to inflation over the year) is deducted since no increase in output has actually occurred because of this. A residual error figure is included since there will be discrepancies between each of the methods due to statistical collection errors:

Incomes from employment
\+ Incomes from profits
\+ Incomes from rents, etc.
\- Stock appreciation
\- Residual error
= *Gross domestic product*

Expenditure Method

Here total spending on final output under different headings is measured. Some goods will be semifinished or finished but not yet sold, so these are added as 'increase in stocks and works in progress'. Exported goods have been produced in the UK but not bought here, so their value is added. Imports have been bought in the UK but not produced here, so their value is deducted. Finally, taxes artificially inflate prices and subsidies undervalue the underlying production costs, so these are deducted and added respectively to move from market prices to factor costs. Once again a residual error is included.

Consumer's expenditure
\+ Government final consumption
\+ Gross domestic fixed capital formation
\+ Value of increase in stocks and works in progress
\+ Exports of goods and services
\- Imports of goods and services
\- Residual error
= *Gross domestic product (at market prices)*
\- Expenditure taxes
\+ Subsidies
= *Gross domestic product (at factor cost)*

Output Method

Outputs of different sectors of the economy are valued, taking care to avoid double-counting. This occurs where the output of one industry is the input to another. Double-counting can be avoided by measuring the value of final, rather than intermediate output.

+ Value of outputs from different sectors of economy
= *Gross domestic product*

From GDP to National Income

Gross domestic product values the flow of goods and services produced in the UK. Some income arises from investments and possessions owned abroad, and thus an adjustment for net property income from abroad is made to GDP to calculate GNP Finally, some investment spending occurs to replace worn-out machinery. Net National Product (NNP) or national income deducts this amount (capital depreciation). These final calculations are summarised below:

Gross domestic product
+ Net property income from abroad
= *Gross national product*
- Capital consumption
= *Net national product (national income)*

Real and Money National Income

When national income figures are compared over two different time periods, the effects of inflation can be misleading. Money national income of national income at current prices includes the effects of inflation. Real national income or national income at constant prices has had the effects of inflation removed.

Leisure and Tourism Contribution to GNP

Table 9.1 gives an indication of the importance of the leisure and tourism sector to the UK economy. From the data it can be seen that nearly 24 per cent of average expenditure in 1996 to 1997 was on leisure items. Table 9.1 shows the difficulties in defining leisure. The Office for National Statistics has two

Table 9.1
Average Household Expenditure 1996-97 (£ per week)

Category	*£*	*£*
Housing	49.10	
Fuel and power	13.35	
Food and non-alcoholic drinks	55.15	
Restaurant and café meals		*7.81*
Take-away meals eaten at home		*2.43*
Alcoholic drink	12.41	
Tobacco	6.07	
Clothing and footwear	18.27	
Household goods	26.74	
Pets and pet food		*2.78*
Household services	16.63	
Telephone		*5.46*
Personal goods and services	11.64	
Motoring	41.20	
Fares and other travel costs	7.45	
Air and other travel and transport		*3.51*
Bicycles, boats, purchase and repair		*1.25*
Leisure goods	15.17	
Books, maps, diaries		*1.14*
Newspapers		*2.01*
Magazines and periodicals		*0.84*
TVs, video, computers and audio equipment		*6.08*
Sports and camping equipment		*0.66*
Toys and hobbies		*1.61*
Photography and camcorders		*0.94*
Horticultural goods, plants, flowers		*1.89*
Leisure services	33.95	
Cinema and theatre		*0.87*
Sports admissions and subscriptions		*2.19*
TV, video and satellite rental, TV licences		*3.26*
Miscellaneous entertainment		*1.04*
Educational and training expenses		*4.55*
Holidays in U K		*2.41*
Holidays abroad		*7.45*
Other incidental holiday expenses		*3.37*
Gambiling payments		*3.82*
Cash gifts, donations		*5.00*
Miscellaneous	2.21	
Leisure items		**72.36**
All expenditure groups	**309.07**	

Source: Adapted from Office for National Statistics: *Family Spending: A Report on the 1996-97 Family Expenditure Survey.*

categories–leisure goods and leisure services. Some other leisure items have also been highlighted, and clearly some aspects of 'motoring' and 'clothing and footwear' will include leisure expenditure.

Care needs to be exercised in interpreting the contribution of leisure to national income using Table 9.1 alone. The exhibit records UK household expenditure, but as the earlier section on GNP calculation explained, exports of leisure goods and services need to be added to this figure and imports deducted. Imported•services are clearly an important part of holiday expenditure. Similarly, some leisure activity does not involve an activity which is bought and sold in the market. Neither informal sports games not DIY labour are measured in GNP statistics because of this, although both result in services enjoyed or value added.

Leisure and Tourism Employment

The demand for labour is a derived demand. Labour is demanded when a good or service is demanded. Employment in the leisure and tourism sector is thus directly related to expenditure on goods and services provided by the sector. Figure 9.2 shows the possible outcomes of leisure and tourism spending.

Some expenditure will be on imported goods or services and will therefore create employment overseas. UK leisure and tourism goods and services will be supplied as a result of domestic expenditure and exports. The resulting derived demand of labour will also depend upon the price of labour relative to other factors of production and the possible technical mix of factors of production able to provide the goods or services. For example, if the price of labour rises, producers will attempt to use more machinery (capital) where this is technically possible.

Sector Employment

Table 9.2 shows recent employment trends in leisure and tourism service industries.

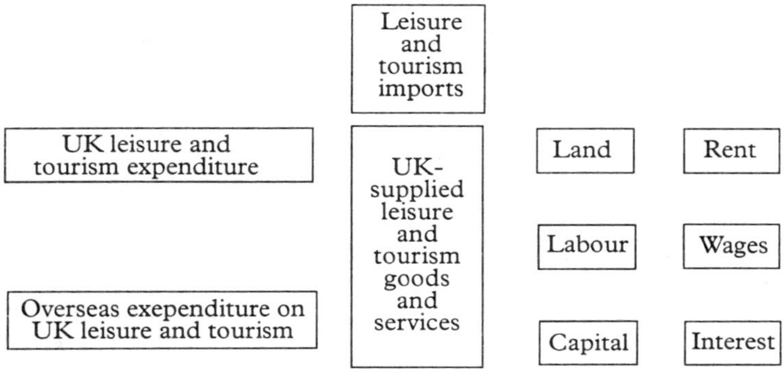

Figure 9.2 : Demand for labour in leisure and tourism secor.

Table 9.2
Employment in Leisure and Tourism Service Industries (GB) in thousands)

	1990	*1995*	*1996*	*1997*
Hotels and other tourist accommodation	289	293	307	311
Restaurants, cafés, etc.	302	319	333	356
Public house, bars and clubs	446	396	391	369
Travel agencies/Tour operators	72	79	83	75
Libraries, museums, galleries and other cultural activities	72	73	74	71
Sports and other recreational activities	290	298	312	297
Total	1471	1459	1499	1419

Source: Adapted from Office for National Statistics, *Labour Market Trends.*

Table 9.3 shows the total number employed and unemployed during the same period.

Table 9.3
UK Employed and Unemployed (millions)

	1990	*1991*	*1992*	*1993*	*1994*	*1995*	*1996*	*1997*	*1998**	*1999*
Employees in employment	22.9	22.3	21.8	21.6	21.5	21.9	22.3	22.8	23.2	
Unemployed	1.6	2.3	2.8	2.9	2.6	2.3	2.1	1.6	1.4	

Source: Adapted from Office for National Statistics, *Economic Trends.*
*Estimated

The general employment picture shown in Table 9.3 is one of rising employment (and falling unemployment) in response to the boom in the economy in the late 1980s, with employment prospects worsening again towards 1992 as a result of the recessions and a fall in consumers' expenditure. The total employment in leisure and tourism services records in Table 9.2 mirrors this national trend, but within the data, numbers employed in libraries, museums, galleries, sports and other recreational services have increased despite the recession of the early 1990s. The figures also show that unemployment has been a persistent feature of the UK economy in recent years, with unemployment not dipping below 1.4 million.

It is more difficult to extract employment in leisure manufacturing from published data, as many of the industrial classifications used by the Department of Employment include leisure and non-leisure items.

Table 9.4 shows the employment totals for the services and manufacturers sectors in the UK with specific data for paper, printing, publishing and recording media, and hotels and restaurants.

Table 9.4
Employees by Sector in the UK (thousands)

	1985	*1987*	*1989*	*1991*	*1993*	*1995*
Manufacturing sector	5002	4815	4851	4319	3913	4026
Service sector	14428	14897	15929	16187	16180	16606
Paper, printing, publishing and recording media	463	459	472	462	445	465
Hotels and restaurant	1004	1009	1176	1209	1162	1230

Source: Adapted from Office for National Statistics, *Labour Market Trends.*

Whereas employment in the services sector has grown in importance, manufacturing employment in the UK has shown a long-term decline. This is caused by two factors. First, technological progress enables productivity increases in manufacturing and thus the ratio of labour input to output declines. Second, manufacturing has been subject to intense competition from overseas where low labour costs in particular result in increased import penetration in UK markets. This is known as deindustrialisation.

Wages

Wages in any particular labour market will be determined by the demand and supply of labour. The supply of labour to some parts of the leisure and tourism (for example, hotels and catering) sector is largely unskilled and this exerts a downward pressure on wages. This is illustrated in Table 9.5 which shows the total wage costs per hour of selected industries. The costs shown include all employer costs (training and national insurance, for example) and thus are roughly 20 per cent higher than wages received.

Table 9.5
Average Gross Weekly Earnings (GB, 1998) (£)

Industry	*Manual*	*Non-manual*
Manufacturing	330	454
Hotels and restaurants	199	335
Financial intermediation	373	522
Education	256	420

Source: Adapted from Office for National Statistics, *Labour Market Trends.*

Leisure and Tourism Multipliers

The analysis of data in the previous sections has looked at tourism and leisure contributions to national income and the economy at a single point in time. This is termed as 'static' analysis. However, consideration of Figure 9.1 shows that tourism and leisure expenditure, like any other form of expenditure, also has 'dynamic' effects due to the circular flow of income and expenditure in the economy. The initial effects of expenditure will generate income but there will be further effects as that income generates expenditure and so on.

Figure 9.3 illustrates the circular flow of income and expenditure derived from Figure 9.1 Assume now that there is an investment into this closed system of £100000 on a new leisure complex. Firms will hire factors of production to the value of £100000 and therefore national income, measured at point A, will rise by £100000. However, the effects of the investment do not stop there. The workers who earned money from building the complex will spend their money in shops and bars, etc. Thus, the incomes of shop and bar owners will rise. They in turn will spend their incomes. In other words, a circular flow of income and expenditure will take place. The investment expenditure sets in motion a dynamic process, and the total extra income passing point A will exceed the initial £100000. This is known as the multiplier effect.

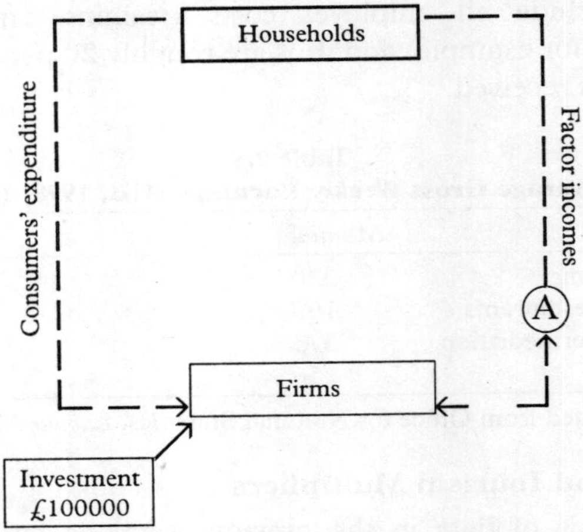

Fig. 9.3: Investment and the circular flow of income.

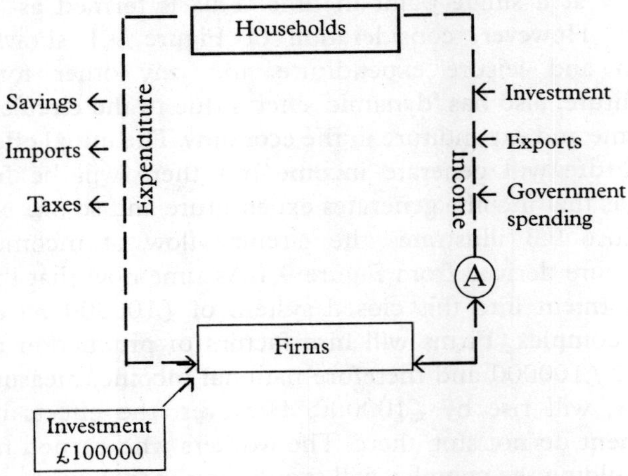

Fig. 9.4: Circular flow with injections and leakages.

In the closed system illustrated by Figure 9.3, the effect would be perpetual and infinite, with the extra expenditure circulating round and round the system. In the real world however there are points at which money can leave and enter the system. This is illustrated in Figure 9.4.

The key leakages or withdrawals for the economy are savings, imports and taxes. Savings represents funds retained by households and firms. Imports result in expenditure flowing overseas, and taxes represent money taken out of the circular flow of income by the government in the form of income tax, VAT and corporation tax, for example.

On the other hand, there are also injections or flows into the circular flow of income. These are investment, exports resulting in money from overseas entering the circular flow, and government spending including for example pensions and unemployment benefit. Clearly there are often strong relationships between specific leakages and injections. To keep the model simple, injections and leakages are located neatly around the system but in reality they occur in many different places.

The existence of leakages means that money is flowing out of the economy during each cycle. So, in the example of the £100000 investment in a leisure complex, perhaps £10000 might be saved by workers, £5000 spend on imported goods, and £10000 taken in taxation. Thus, the initial effect on national income measured at point A in Figure 9.4 is £100000. Out of this, £25000 will be lost in leakages from the economy, leaving £75000 to recirculate, adding another £75000 to national income at point A. This process then continues, but with each cycle becoming smaller. It should be seen that the size of the multiplier effect will depend upon the amount of the original injection under examination and the leakages from the economy.

The Keynesian Multiplier

The Keynesian multiplier can now be formally analysed. The multiplier (*k*) shows the amount by which a change in expenditure (ΔEXP) in an economy leads to a change in national income (Δγ):

$$\Delta EXP \times k = \Delta \gamma$$

Thus, if an increase in investment on a leisure complex of £100000 led to a final increase in national income of £400000, then the multiplier would have a value of 4.

The multiplier can be illustrated by reference to Table 9.6 and Figure 9.5.

Investment in the leisure complex of £100000 is made and national income at point A is raised by £100000. In round 2, leakages consist of £10000 in savings, £10000 in taxes and £5000 in imports, leaving £75000 in domestic expenditure to recirculate round the circular flow. An extra £75000 is therefore added to national income at point A. In round 3 leakages consist of £7500 in savings, £7500 in taxes and £3750 in imports, leaving £56250 in domestic expenditure. This process continues, and the leakages reduce the value of extra domestic expenditure and national income at every round. In fact, the extra amounts of national income tend towards zero. If the additions to national income in column 6, for years 1-*n* (where *n* = the year in which the effect has dwindled to near zero) ware added up, they would sum to £40000, thus giving a value for the multiplier of 4.

There is also a formula for calculating the multiplier:

$k = 1/MPL$

where *MPL* = the marginal propensity to leak (the proportion of extra income that leaks out of the economy).

Table 9.6
Multiplier Rounds

Round	ΔS	ΔT	ΔM	ΔEXP	ΔY
1				100000	100000
2	10000	10000	5000	75000	75000
3	7500	7500	3750	56250	56250
4	5625	5625	2812.50	42187.50	42187.50
5	4218.75	4218.75	2109.36	31640.63	31640.63
6	3164.06	3164.06	1582.03	23730.47	23730.47
7	2373.05	2373.05	1186.52	17797.85	17797.85
8	1779.76	1779.76	889.89	13348.39	13348.39
9-*n*	...	...	...	...	...
Total				400000	400000

Note: Rounds 9-*n* represent the remaining multiplier rounds. *S*=Savings; *T* = taxes; *M* = imports; *EXP* = expenditure; *Y* = income; *D* = change in.

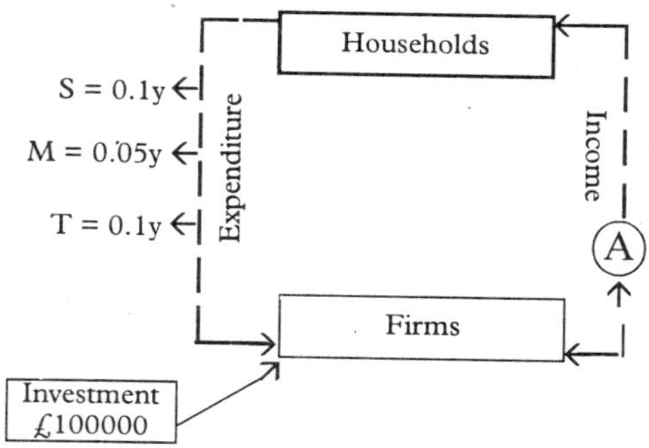

Figure 9.5 : The multiplier round. S = Savings; M = imports; T = taxes; Y = income.

$$MPL = MPS + MPM + MPT$$

where *MPS* = marginal propensity to save (the proportion of extra income saved), *MPM* = marginal propensity to spend on imports (the proportion of extra income spent on imports) and *MPT* = marginal propensity to be taxed (the proportion of extra income taken in taxes).

In the above example, *MPS* = 1.1Y, *MPM* = 0.05 Y and *MPT* = 0.1 Y, where Y = income. Therefore:

$$Y = 1/(0.1 + 0.05 + 0.1)$$
$$Y = 1/0.25$$
$$Y = 4$$

Tourism Multipliers

Considerable research has been done into the impact of tourism and leisure expenditure using multiplier techniques. The aim is to assess impact on incomes, output and employment at national, regional and local levels. This is clearly an important issue for governments in assessing the contribution of such developments to economic activity. The main multipliers developed for impact analysis are:

- the output multiplier
- the income multiplier
- the employment multiplier
- the government revenue multiplier

Table 9.7
Multiplier and Expenditure Impacts

Value of multiplier	*Leakages from the economy*	*Impact of expenditure on income*
High	Low	High
Low	High	Low

Taking the case of the tourism income multiplier (TIM), values vary according to leakages, as summarised in Table 9.7, and actual results include Canada (TIM = 2.5), UK (TIM = 1.8), Iceland (TIM = 0.6) and Edinburagh (TIM = 0.4).

Exhibit 9.1 discusses tourism multipliers in Scotland.

Leisure and Tourism Inflation

Inflation can be defined as a rise in the general level of prices or a fall in the purchasing power of money. It is measured by the Retail Price Index (RPI). If one country has a faster rate of inflation than that of other countries, it can cause a decline in international competitiveness. This is likely to affect firms producing leisure products for the export market, and countries which rely on tourism. It is less likely to affect firms in leisure services since customers rarely have the option to seek lower prices overseas for these.

Constructing a Tourism Destination Price Index

It is possible to construct a Tourism Destination Price Index (TDPI) using a similar methodology to that used to construct

Exhibit 9.1 : Small is Beautiful

The Scottish Office has been studying the relationship between size of tourism establishments and effects on local income and spending. Its findings are that smaller organisations are more beneficial to local economies because the centralised buying activities of large organisations take spending out of the local area.

The Scottish Tourism Multiplier Study on Edinburgh made the following findings. In 1990, it is estimated that domestic and overseas tourists spent £276m in Edinburgh. For every £1000 spent by UK-resident tourists in Edinburg, approximately £346 in income is generated locally and £127 in income is generated in the rest of Scotland. It takes about £27000 of spending by domestic tourists to create one new job in the city.

Source: Scottish Office.

the general RPI. Table 9.8 gives an example of such an index. The steps are as follows (with rows and columns referring to Table 9.8):

Table 9.8
Tourism Price Index, Example (pesetas)

Item	*Weight (W)*	*1996*		*1997*		*1998*	
		Price (P)	*P × W*	*Price (P)*	*P×W*	*Price (P)*	*P×W*
Babycham (25 cl)	0.4	200	80	220	88	250	100
Beer (0.51)	4.0	190	760	195	780	200	800
Three-course meal	11.6	800	9280	880	10208	950	11020
...	...	...	...	...	...	...	...
...	...	...	...	...	...	...	...
Total			50107		52612		56119
Index multiple				0.0019957291			
Index			100		105		112

Notes: Item = row 1, column 1; the dots in rows 6 and 7 denote the rest of the basket of goods.

- First it is necessary to define the population for whom the index is intended. This might be a specific index for golfers or skiers.
- Next an expenditure survey must be conducted to establish the spending patterns of the target population, ensuring that a representative sample of the target population is surveyed.
- From this two important findings should emerge–first a 'basket of goods' (and services) that lists the items bought by tourists can be compiled (column 1), and second the relative importance of each item can be gauged from the expenditure survey and each item given a weighting accordingly. For example, if an expenditure survey in Magaluf, Majorca showed 10 times more beer to be consumed than Babycham, then beer would be assigned a weighting 10 times more than that for Babycham (column 2). Thus, if beer and Babycham both rose in price by 20 per cent, the effect of Babycham on the TDPI would be less than the beer effect.

- A survey of the prices of the basket of goods is then conducted (column 3).
- Expenditure on each item is determined by mutiplying its price by its weighting (column 4).
- The total expenditure on the basket of goods is recorded (row 8).
- This amount is then converted to a index number with base 100 by using a multiplier (row 9), and this becomes the base year reading. (For example, if the expenditure total is £50, a multiplier of 2 is needed to convert the result to 100.)
- The basket of goods is priced at regular intervals (columns 5 and 7), with expenditure totals (row 8) being converted to an index number (row 10) using the multiplier established in the base year (row 9).

Table 9.9

Tourism Price Index (Exchange Rate-adjusted)

	1996	*1997*	*1998*
Total (Pts)	50107	52612	56119
£1 = ? Pesetas	198	240	251
Total (£s)	253.06	219.22	223.53
Index multiple		0.39516	
Index	100	86.54	88.22

The index resulting from this exercise (Table 9.8) gives a picture of tourism inflation in the local currency. It is possible to adjust the index to reflect exchange rate conditions in different countries. Thus, whilst Table 9.8 measures tourism inflation for a Spanish visitor to a Spanish destination, Table 9.9 shows how the index can be adapted for a British visitor.

Table 9.9 uses the expenditure data from row 8 of Table 9.8. This is then converted to an equivalent in the currency under consideration (sterling in this example). A new index multiple is calculated to convert the raw expenditure figure to an index number with base 100. Comparison of the two tables shows the importance of considering exchange rate fluctuations when comparing prices between tourist destinations.

It must be remembered that any tourism price index represents an average picture, and individuals will be affected differently according to their particular expenditure patterns. Care must also be exercised in the collecting of data. There must be consistency of sources, otherwise the index will be distorted by changes in prices which result for example by moving from a local store to a supermarket.

Table 9.10 shows the relative sterling prices of commonly consumed leisure goods and services in different contries.

Table 9.10
International Price Comparison for Leisure Goods and Services, 1998 (£)

	UK	*USA*	*Italy*	*Germany*	*France*	*Denmark*
Compact disc	13.38	9.56	12.14	11.08	13.08	11.84
Paperback book	5.94	4.22	6.17	5.40	3.53	8.11
Cinema ticket	4.45	4.44	4.07	4.13	4.70	4.62
22-inch colour TV	387.46	201.19	375.23	307.96	351.46	501.83
Radio cassette recorder	49.99	34.67	51.49	50.52	57.48	60.18
Restaurant dinner	19.99	16.78	17.38	17.69	17.28	21.17
Drink at bar	3.29	3.29	2.58	4.20	4.90	5.59

Notes: Restaurant dinner for one, bar drink is double measure of spirits.
Source: Adapted from ECA International.

Table 9.11
UK Retail Price Indices (January 1987 = 100)

	July 1994	*July 1998*	*July 2000*
All items	144	163	
Travel and leisure	146	164	
Audiovisual goods	75	56	
Tapes and discs	113	120	
Toys, photographic and sport goods	121	119	
Books and newspapers	159	187	
Gardening products	141	142	
Television licences and rentals	118	130	
Entertainment and other recreation	193	232	

Source: Adapted from Office for National Statistics, *Labour Market Trends*.

Table 9.11 shows some of the components of the RPI for the UK. It can be seen that inflation in the travel and leisure sector as a whole has been similar to that of the general level of inflation. However, within the sector audiovisual equipment prices have actually fallen whilst entertainment and other recreation prices have shown steep rises.

Government Policy

Income and Employment

Governments throughout the world see leisure and tourism as a source of employment, particularly where structural changes in the economy have led to job losses, as Exhibit 9.2 shows.

Government policies to promote employment may include the following:

Demand Management

Where there is unemployment throughout the economy, some economists advocate government stimulation of aggregate demand so as to induce more production and thus employment. Aggregate demand may be stimulated through tax cuts, increased government spending and interest rate cuts. The major drawback to such a policy is its tendency to encourage inflation.

Export-led Policies

Overseas expenditure on leisure and tourism products can contribute to employment. Government policy here includes expenditure on the BTA which promotes the UK overseas and thus overseas demand for UK leisure and tourism services.

A low exchange rate also assists exports of services and leisure goods.

Wages and Conditions of Employment

The Conservative government had a policy of 'flexible labour markets'. The Conservative government view was that high wages, complex labour laws and unionisation act as a disincentive to employers to create jobs. To this end wage councils which enforce minimum wages were abolished, and

Exhibit 9.2 : Artistic Revival for Cill Rialaig

Cill Rialaig is a deserted village on the western fringes of Europe in County Kerry, Ireland. It never really recovered from the nineteenth century potato famine and the last inhabitants left in the 1950s. Plans for economic regeneration are being made based on the model of St Ives in Cornwall, England. It is hoped to encourage a community of artists and to build a £1 million art gallery, modelled on Cornwall's Tate.

Visiting artists are encouraged by a policy of rent-free accommodation and renovation of buildings is being helped by artists donating a finished picture to the project which is sold in the newly built local arts centre.

Mr. O'Connell is typical of those who have found employment through the scheme. He works at the Arts Centre making picture frames. This is part of a government-sponsored back-to-work scheme for the long-term unemployed. He hopes to become self-employed when the government scheme runs out.

An application has been made to the Tourist Board, Arts Council and Ministry of Arts for funds to finance an international art gallery in nearby Waterville to attract major touring exhibitions more visitors. Local doctor Dery Gibson supports the scheme saying, 'We went through the eighties with everyone emigrating. Post offices and garda stations were closing. It was a very depressing time. An idea like this could revitalize the place and bring families back. We don't want hordes of campers and caravans, but if people could come and enjoy the peace and quiet and mix that with a bit of culture it would hold them in the area instead of them just passing through.

Source: The author from article in the *Guardian*, 1998.

the UK opted out of EU labour laws, including paternity leave for fathers. A succession of law curbing trade union activity was passed in the 1980s. The Labour government, elected in 1997, has introduced a minimum wage and has brought UK labour laws in line with that of the EU.

Project Assistance

The government also considers direct assistance with projects on an individual basis, particularly where a project can be shown to bring employment to areas of high unemployment. There was for example considerable competition between France and the UK over inducements offered to lure EuroDisney to each country. The EU also has a regional fund which can be a source of financial assistance.

Inflation

Governments of countries with comparatively high rates of inflation may utilise counter-inflationary policy. However, it is important first to diagnose the cause of inflation.

Causes of Inflation

The causes of inflation can be divided into the categories of cost-push, demand-pull, monetary, taxation and expectations.

Cost-push inflation occurs when increased production costs are passed on as price rises. These can include first wage increases which outstrip productivity increases. Second increased raw material prices can be important. If raw materials are imported, a fall in the exchange rate can increase their local currency price.

Demand-pull inflation tends to occur when an economy is growing too fast. It arises because the aggregate demand in the economy exceeds the aggregate supply in the economy and therefore prices are bid up. Labour for example may become scarce, putting an upward pressure on wages.

Too rapid an increase in the money supply of an economy can cause an increase on consumer credit which can stimulate demand-pull inflation and accommodate cost-push inflation.

Increases in indirect taxes such as VAT will have an effect on prices, whilst if people expect inflation to rise, they will often seek to protect their living standards by higher wage demands. These of course will then cause the very inflation that people are seeking to avoid.

Counter Inflationary Policy

Government counter inflationary policy will affect the economic environment of leisure and tourism organisations.

Cost-push inflation may be tackled by a high exchange rate policy. Whilst this may be good for tacking inflation, it makes firms' exports less competitive.

Wage rises may be tackled by government-imposed incomes policy to curb pay increases. This may cause a deterioration in industrial relations.

Deflationary policy may be used to tackle demand-pull inflation. This may entail increasing interest rates to curb consumer borrowing, or increased taxes to reduce consumer spending. Either way, whilst inflation may be tackled, firms will suffer a general contraction in demand.

High interest rates are sometimes also used to curb overexpansion of the money supply be reducing the demand for borrowing.

Review of Key Terms

- Macroeconomics = the study of the national economy.
- National income = a measure of the total level of economic activity which takes place in an economy over a year.
- GDP = gross domestic product.
- GNP = gross national product.
- NNP = net national product (national income).
- Money national income = national income calculated at current prices.
- Real national income = national income calculated at constant prices (inflationary element removed).
- Tourism income multiplier (TIM) = exaggerated effect of a change in tourism expenditure on an area's income.
- TDPI = tourism destination price index.
- Basket of goods = typical items bought by a defined group.
- Cost-push inflation = inflation caused by changes in input prices.
- Demand-pull inflation = inflation caused by excess of aggregate demand over aggregate supply.
- Demand management = government policy to influence total demand in an economy.

Data Questions

Task 9.1

Table 9.12 shows retail price indices for selected countries.

Table 9.12
Retails Price Indices (1990 = 100)

	1993	*1994*	*1995*	*1996*	*1997*	*1998**
United Kingdom	116	119	122	125	128	131
Germany	111	114	116	117	119	121
Italy	116	121	128	132	135	138
United States	110	113	116	119	122	123
Japan	106	106	106	106	108	108
Canada	110	110	113	115	117	118

*Estimate.
Source: Adopted from Office for National Statistics, *Labour Market.*

Questions

1. It entrance to Disneyland cost $20 in 1990, and its price has kept pace with inflation, what would a ticket cost in 1998?
2. Why might the retail price index for a country not be a good guide to tourism prices?
3. What other information would you seek before deciding on which countries might be good or bad value to visit?
4. Account for the differing rates of inflation between countries.
5. Why is the Italian rate of inflation likely to fall to German levels post 1999?

Task 9.2: Local Reflections on the Channel Tunnel

The Channel Tunnel is dug, equipped and running. How does local opinion see its effects?

John Ovenden, Labour leader, and Allison Wainman, Liberal Democrat leader on Kent County Council, made a joint statement reflecting on possible impacts, on the official tunnel opening.

'For Kent, the tunnel is a mixed blessing. There is no doubt that many people in Kent have paid and will continue to pay a high price in terms of the environmental effect of the project.

Equally, traditional cross-channel operators, who provide many jobs for Kent people, face a real challenge, although there is every sign that they are responding positively.

However, we are determined to maximise the benefits for Kent of the tunnel. By opening up transport corridors at the heart of Europe, it represents an opportunity too good to be missed at a time when the county is well-placed to take advantage. For too long, parts of the county have been in the economic doldrums'.

It is certainly true that Kent has had its fair share of economic misery in recent years. Agricultural employment in the county, renowned for hop growing and orchards, has suffered a steady long-term decline in the face of mechanisation. It is easy to forget that Kent once had a coal industry which closed in the face of cheap imports in the 1980s. Defence cuts and the peace dividend have been responsible for the decline of Chatham whose prosperity has rested on its naval dockyards. Such is the level of unemployment in north and east Kent that they have gained assisted-areas status. Thanet is eligible for assistance from the EU on account of its 17 per cent unemployment rate.

Consultants estimate that nearly 2000 jobs will have been created by the Channel Tunnel by 1996. However, it is also estimated that about 15000 people are employed in jobs related to port activities in Kent and that a net loss of 3000 of these jobs will result from the impact of the tunnel on ferry services by 1996.

More difficult to estimate is the employment effects of the tunnel on the tourism industry. The county is second only to London as a destination for overseas visitors, who spent £132m in 1992. It is likely that the tunnel will boost this figure.

Source: The author, from news cuttings, 6 May, 1994.

Questions

1 What general employment conditions are described in the article for Kent?

2. Describe the employment effects of the Channel Tunnel using the following headings:
   (a) Direct (employment provided by the project itself).
   (b) Displacement (employment lost because of the project's effects).
   (c) Indirect (employment gained or lost by the project's effects).

3. What are the likely multiplier effects on Kent of:
   (a) the construction phase of the tunnel?
   (b) The operation phase of the tunnel?

Task 9.3

Table 9.13 shows consumers' expenditure on selected leisure items.

Questions

1. What is the significance of the term 'at 1990 market prices'?
2. How would these figures need to be adapted if they were used to help compile GNP?
3. To what extent are such figures on expenditure a guide to changes in the level of employment is each of the areas?

Table 9.13
Consumers' Expenditure at 1990 Market Prices (£m)

	1986	*1988*	*1990*	*1992*	*1994*	*1996*	*1998*
Radio, television and other durable goods	2957	4195	4729	5324	6418	8210	
TV and video hire charges, licence fees and repairs	3145	3197	3204	2991	3127	3009	
Sports goods, toys, games and camping equipment	2506	2838	3443	3398	3881	4397	
Betting and gaming	2924	3124	3116	2914	3292	5083	
Newspapers and magazines	3197	3219	3286	2964	3109	2898	

Source: Adapted from Office for National Statistics, *Annual Abstract of Statistics*.

Task 9.4: The Death of Inflation?

The Centre for Economics and Business Research (CEBR) issued a forecast in December 1998 that the UK economy will move into a period of 'negative inflation'. It has warned that by 2002 retail prices will be falling by about 0.2 per cent per year. This would reverse the postwar trend of inflation that accelerated in the 1970s after sharp rises in oil prices and an intense period of wage-price spirals. Much behaviour in the economy has been based on expectations of continued inflation. This includes investment in property and a readiness to use credit for the purchase of goods. Chief executive of CEBR, Professor Douglas McWilliams, said: 'This will be a new world for most people working today. In the future we will no longer be able to think in terms of the annual wage and price increases.'

Negative inflation will result if oil and commodity prices continue to fall, if world trade is hit by recessions in major economies, and if companies are left with large stocks of unsold goods. Janice Clark, an economist with CEBR, predicts that once negative inflation starts, a prolonged cycle of falling prices may follow. Producers are likely to want to compensate for reduced prices by reducing wages and this will enable prices to fall further but also reduce demand putting further downward pressure on prices.

Some of the consequences of negative inflation may include:

- A fall in interest rates (CEBR expect these to fall to 2.4 per cent by 2002).
- Pay cuts.
- Consumers delaying purchases in the hope of lower prices.
- A collapse in property prices.
- A 1930s style period of depression.

Source: The author, from reports from the Centre for Economics and Business Research.

Questions

1. How accurate was this forecast? Discuss reasons for this.
2. What is the difference between a recession and negative inflation?
3. 'Negative inflation–opportunity or thereat to the leisure industry?' Discuss with reference to the ways in which opportunities could be exploited and threats successfully managed.

10

INVESTMENT IN THE PRIVATE SECTOR FOR TOURISM

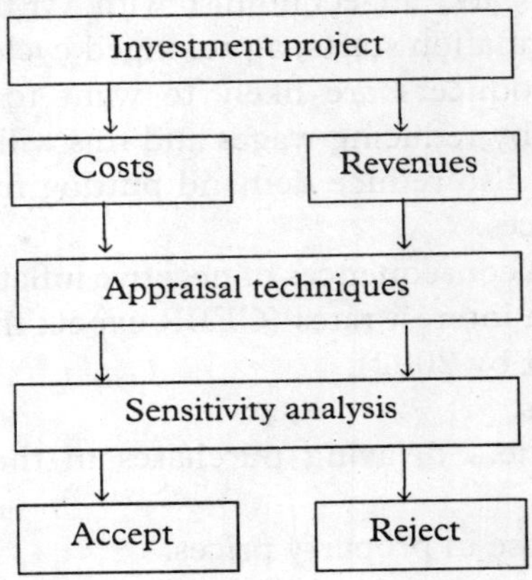

Objectives

With hindsight it is not difficult to analyse the factors that have made some investment projects in the leisure and tourism sector such successes and others such dismal failures. The failures include films (*Raise the Titanic*), transport systems (Virgin Rail) and electronic games (Sega Saturn). The successes include projects as diverse as films (*Titanic*), visitor attractions (Port Aventura), and electronic games (Sony Play Station).

However, at the planning stage, it is much more difficult to forecast the success of investments, largely because of the uncertainty surrounding the future. This chapter seeks to define the meaning of investment, consider how potential investment projects are appraised and stress the shortcomings of quantitative techniques.

By studying this chapter students will be able to:

- define and distinguish between different types of investment,
- analyse the factors which affect an investment decision,
- utilise techniques for investment appraisal,
- understand the uncertainty surrounding investment appraisal,
- analyse the effects of investment on the economy,
- evaluate government policy with regard to investment.

Definition and Examples

In general usage people use the term 'investment' to include bank and building society deposits and the purchase of stocks and shares. Economists are more specific in their use of the term. Investment may be defined as expenditure on capital goods and working capital.

Capital goods can be contrasted with consumer goods. The latter are produced because of the direct satisfaction they yield (e.g. food, CDs, clothes), whilst the former are produced because they improve efficiency of production. Fixed capital goods therefore consist of buildings, plant and machinery, and in the leisure and tourism sector examples include hotel buildings, computer reservation and booking systems, aircraft and golf-ball making machinery. The total expenditure on such items is recorded as 'gross domestic fixed capital formation' in government statistics.

Working capital consists of stocks of raw-materials, semi-manufactured goods and manufactured goods which have not yet been sold. Manufacturers monitor stocks of unsold products closely and these tend to be the key signals in a market economy to reduce or increase production. Working capital is an essential part of production, although modern 'just-in-time' production techniques have reduced the need for large stocks of raw materials and components to be held in factories. Expenditure on these items is recorded in government statistics as 'increase in stocks and work in progress'. Table 10.1 illustrates recent data for the UK showing gross domestic fixed capital formation.

It can be seen that gross fixed capital formation increased in the period 1987 to 1989, fell in 1990 and did not recover its 1988 level until 1995. It has steadily risen between 1993 and 1998.

Figure 10.1 shows the value of new investment projects in the leisure and tourism sector. It shows a similar picture to the total investment figures, reaching a peak in 1989 and falling in the following period, and demonstrates the effects of recession on investment.

Investment can also be divided into gross investment and net investment. Gross investment includes all investment, including that which is for replacement of work-out machinery, whilst net investment only includes investment that adds to a country's capital stock.

Net investment ≐ gross investment – depreciation

Table 10.1
UK Investment 1987–1993 (£m at Constant 1995 Prices)

Year	*Gross domestic fixed capital formation*
1987	100520
1988	115362
1989	122158
1990	119368
1991	109000
1992	108246
1993	109127
1994	107042
1995	116360
1996	122042
1997	129645
1998*	135104

*Estimate

Source: Adapted from Office for National Statistics: *Monthly Digest of Statistics.*

Factors Affecting Investment

Investment in the private sector is undertaken to increase profitability. Since we assume that the motive of private sector

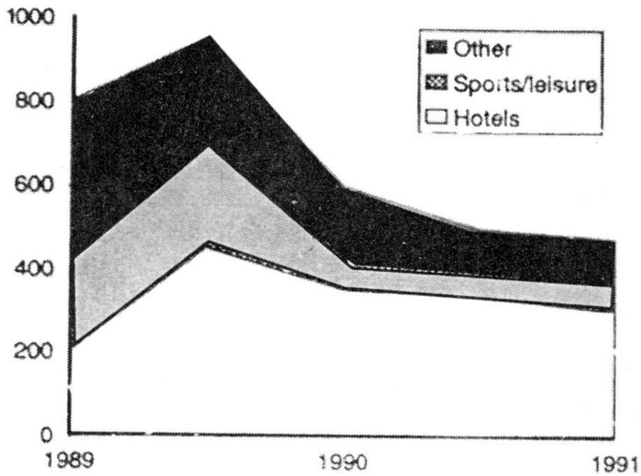

Figure 10.1: Value of new leisure and tourism investment projects commenced in England (£m).

organisations is the maximisation of profits, such organisations will seek to invest in those projects which yield the highest return.

Exhibit 10.1: Holiday Inn: Europe

The UK brewery and leisure group Bass plc has announced new investment plans for extending its Holiday inn hotels into Europe.

Its chosen strategy is to expand mainly by franchising, and to extend its presence in the budget market. The vehicle for this is the Holiday Inn Express concept aimed at price-conscious travellers.

By avoiding costly city-centre sites and concentrating instead on roadside locations, the investment cost to franchisees is expected to range between £28000 and £30000 per room and rooms are likely to cost an average of £35 a night.

Both of these figures are substantially less than those associated with standard Holiday inns.

Source: The author.

Investment projects will incur planning, construction and running costs and yield revenue when in operation. Thus, the profitability of an investment project can be analysed by investigating its costs and revenue. Exhibit 10.1 gives a rough idea of the costs and revenue for a hotel development.

Cost of Investment

The main costs of an investment will be:

- planning costs
- costs of capital goods
- cost of financing investment
- running costs of the investment

Planning Costs

The planning costs of an investment include consultancy costs for technical feasibility, market research, competitor scanning, financial appraisal and overall project planning. For large-scale projects, planning costs can be considerable and add to the overall project timetable. The British Airports Authority (BAA) has been planning a substantial investment in a new passenger terminal–terminal 5–at Heathrow Airport. Table 10.2 shows the original timetable for the project as envisaged in 1992. It can be seen that the planing, consultation and enquiry phase represents an equivalent 5-year period to the construction phase, doubling the project timetable to 10 years.

Exhibit 10.2 shows that by 1999, the project was already 4 years behind schedule.

Table 10.2
Terminal 5 Timetable

Year	*Projected stage*
1992	Local consultations
1992	Submission of planning application
1994	Start of public planning inquiry
1995	End of public planning inquiry
1997	Government decision expected
	Subject to planning approval being granted
1997	Start of construction
2001	Completion of phase 1 construction
2002	Opening of phase 1
2016	Terminal reaches maximum capacity

Source: BAA (1992).

Exhibit 10.2 High Costs of Terminal Failure

1999: If things had gone according to plan, BAA's Terminal 5 (T5) would by now be a busy construction site of cranes, half-completed buildings, and road links. The fact that the site is still occupied by the Perry Oaks Sludge Works demonstrates how far the project has slipped behind schedule. The year 2001' was to have seen the completion of phase 1 of the project, but it will now be the year when the government gives its final decision on whether the project is allowed to go ahead. This will push back the opening of phase 1 from 2002 to 2006, if the project is allowed.

The main delay to the project has been the public enquiry which in the event has taken 3 years to hear the evidence of the BAA, local authorities, environmental campaigners and other interest groups. The overall project has an estimated cost of Euros 2.6 billion. But the delays to the project mean that the planning and preparation costs, which have to be paid even if the project is eventually rejected, have now reached Euros 360 million. These costs have been needed to pay for legal teams at the public enquiry, design costs of the building and the cost of land purchase.

BAA insists that Terminal 5 is needed to maintain Heathrow's competitive edge against rival European hubs such as Amsterdam, Frankfurt and Paris. The new terminal would allow passenger numbers to rise from 58 million per year to 80 million. Anti-T5 groups argue that the project would bring about unacceptable levels of congestion and pollution to a densely populated area of West London.

Source: The author, from press reports 1999.

Costs of Capital Goods

The capital costs of an investment are the costs of buildings, plant and machinery. In some case these are known costs, since there is a market in commonly purchased capital goods such as computer systems, vehicles and standard buildings. For more complex investments capital costs can only be estimated in the planning stage and for large construction projects, estimates of costs are notoriously unreliable. The original estimate for building and equipping the Channel Tunnel was £5bn but by 1993 the figure had been revised to £10bn. Such escalations in costs are typical of large construction projects. In the case of the Channel Tunnel, factors such as price increases in materials, increased wages, unforeseen technical difficulties in boring the tunnel, specification changes to improve safety, and legal disputes over costs between Eurotunnel and the construction company Trans-Manche Link (TML) have all added to the increased costs.

Cost of Financing Investment

Finance for investment projects may be found internally out of a company's profits, or externally from the capital markets, for example, through banks or share issues.

External funding by loans carries costs in terms of interest rates that have to paid for the duration of a loan. These interest rates may be fixed or variable. External funding by share issue incurs issue costs but the costs of funding (i.e. the dividend payments to shareholders) are then tied into future profits.

It might appear that internally generated funds do not carry any special costs, since a company does not have to pay interest on its own funds. However, there is an opportunity cost of using internal funds. That is the cost in terms of other uses to which the funds could have been put. A company could put funds on deposit in the money markets and gain interest on such deposits. Thus, even where internal funds are used for investment, a notional interest rate will be used to represent their opportunity cost. In general, higher interest rates will act as a disincentive to investment.

Running Costs of the Investment

The running costs of an investment will include all the other costs of operating the project. These include labour costs, maintenance costs and raw material costs. New technology which reduces running and production costs can be an important cause of investment.

Revenue from Investment

Total revenue from sales resulting from an investment project can be calculated by multiplying the selling price by the quantity sold and thus the main factors affecting the revenue obtained from an investment are:

- price of output

- quantity of output sold
- other factors

Price of Output

The price of the output of an investment project will largely depend on demand and the competition in the market under consideration. In general the less competition, the more power a supplier will have to set price. Where a monopoly or near monopoly exists, price can be producer-determined (but quantity sold will reflect demand). However, potential competitors will move quickly to produce near substitutes where possible, particularly if a premium price is being charged. Where a few producer exist in a market (oligopoly or monopolistic competition), the impact of a new entrant will change the actions of those already in the market and thus lead to unpredictability. In a perfectly competitive market prices will be driven down to reflect the lowest average costs in the industry.

Thus, although a company may have market intelligence about current prices in the market where its investment is to take place, any estimate of prices in future years is likely to be very uncertain. Channel Tunnel prices, for example, have changed considerably between the planning stage and the present. This reflects the changing marketing strategies of competing ferry and airline companies.

Quantity of Output Sold

Quantity sold will be closely related to price charged. However it will also be related to factors including consumers' income, competitive prices and advertising. Figure 10.2 shows forecasts of passenger demand for airports in the South-east of England. These are part of the feasibility study for London Heathrow's Terminal 5. Clearly there are a range of factors, for example environmental pressures, taxes, fuel costs, which might cause the forecasts to be wrong.

Other Factors

Government policy may affect the revenue that derives from an investment project in several ways. First, government taxation

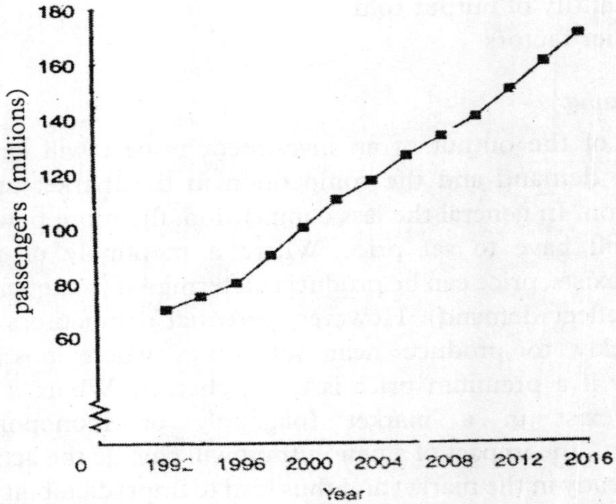

Figure 10.2: Passenger demand forecasts for airports in the South-east.

policy may affect prices (VAT), or spending power (income tax) or profits (corporation tax). Second government legislation may affect the demand for goods, and finally monopolies and mergers legislation may have an impact upon prices that can be charged.

Expectations play a key part in investment decisions. Expectations reflect views about how successful the economy will be in future years. Where investors have a pessimistic view about the future economy they will generally defer investment decisions.

Property development is a prominent feature of much leisure and tourism investment. Whilst rental income is a part of the anticipated revenue from such developments, capital appreciation can also be an important factor. Thus, such developments are often sensitive to expectations about future prices of property.

Above all, the factors surrounding an investment decision are subject to a great deal of uncertainty. Few of the factors have known values. Current interest rates are known, and where an investment obtains funds at fixed rates, this provides a predictable element. However, where funds are obtained at variable interest rates, considerable uncertainty will exist. Similar uncertainty surrounds the final costs of complex capital projects, price of output and demand for the final good or service. These are all subject to changes in the competitive and political, economic, socio-cultural and technological (PEST) environments.

Appraisal Techniques

Having identified the factors affecting the profitability of an investment, these can be used in a variety of quantitative methods to aid decision-making. Investment appraisal reports may appear very authoritative, neatly summarising projects in figures. However, in view of the uncertainties discussed in the previous section, care should be taken to examine the assumption on which appraisals are made. The main appraisal techniques are:

- payback method,
- average rate of return,
- net present value,
- internal rate of return,

Payback Method

This method compares investment projects by measuring the length of time it takes to repay the original investment from the revenues earned. It therefore favours projects which have the earliest payback. The key problems with this method are first that earnings that an investment may make after the payback period are not taken into account, and second revenues are not discounted so earnings within the payback period are given equal weight irrespective of the year they appear in. On the other hand, the sooner the payback, the less a project will be subject to uncertainties, and some companies may see speed of return as a priority over total return. Table 10.3 shows an example of this method and it can be seen that in this example the payback period is 3 years, when the cumulative cash flow reaches zero.

Average Rate of Return

This method calculates the total earnings from an investment and divides this by the number of years of the project's life. This figure is then expressed as a percentage of the capital costs of the project. For example, if an investment project had a total cost of £100000 and earned a total of £50000 over 5 years, the annual earnings would be £10000, which represents an annual average rate of return of £10000/ £100000 or 10 per cent on the capital employed. This method also fails to discount future earnings.

Net Present Value

The net present value method takes into account the fact that future earnings have a lower value than current earnings. For example, £100 today could be invested at a rate of interest of 10 per cent to give £110 in a year's time. Working this backwards, £100 in a year's time is only worth £90.91 today at a rate of interest of 10 per cent. In other words, it has been discounted at a rate of 10 per cent to find its present discounted value. Discount tables exist to assist such calculations but there is also a formula for calculating Present Discounted Value (PDV)

$$\text{PDV} = R_t/(1 + i)^t$$

where R = return, t = year and i = rate of interest or discount rate (expressed as decimal).

Table 10.3
Payback Method of Investment Appraisal (£m)

Year	*0*	*1*	*2*	*3*	*4*
Cost	2.4	0.4	0.4	0.4	0.2
Revenue	0	1.0	1.2	1.4	1.4
Cash flow	-2.4	0.6	0.8	1.0	1.2
Cumulative cash flow	-2.4	-1.8	-1.0	0.0	1.2

Table 10.4
Discounted Cash Flow Method of Investment Appraisal (£m)

Year	*0*	*1*	*2*	*3*	*4*
Net revenue		2.0	5.0	6.0	6.0
Present discounted value of net revenues		1.82	4.13	4.5	4.1

Note: Discount rate = 10 per cent.

Row 2 or Table 10.4 shows the net revenues of a project with an initial capital cost of £16m in years 1–4, and row 3 shows these figures discounted to their present values using a discount rate of 10 per cent.

The net unadjusted revenues sum to £19m and thus the project appears to show a net surplus of £3m. However, the net present value technique compares costs and revenues discounted to their net present values. The total net revenue falls to £14.55m when discounted to present value, and the project shows the following net present value:

Costs at present value	£16.00m
Revenue at present value	£14.55m
Net present value	-£1.45m

This negative figure indicates an unprofitable investment.

Internal Rate of Return

The internal rate of return method also uses discounted cash flow. It calculates the discount rate that would equate the net present value of future earnings of an investment to its initial cost. This rate is called the internal rate of return. An investment will be profitable if its internal rate of return exceeds the rate of interest that has to be paid for borrowing funds for the investment, allowing a margin for risk. A feasibility study into a fixed channel link by Coopers and Lybrand and Setec Economie in 1979 concluded that the internal rate of return on the project would be between 11 and 18 per cent.

When comparing investment projects those with the highest internal rate of return will be selected.

Changes in the Level of Investment

Changes in the level of investment will be caused by changes in the costs and predicted revenues of investments. These factors are summarised in Table 10.5.

The fall in investment in 1990 shown in Table 10.1 and Figure 10.1 can be attributed to high interest rates making the cost of borrowing funds to invest high, falling consumers' expenditure, and poor expectations about the economy in the medium-term. Falling demand leaves machinery underutilised and thus there is little need for new machinery.

Table 10.5
Factors Causing Changes in Investment

	Investment conditions	
	Good	*Poor*
Rate of interest	Low	High
Capital costs predicatble	Yes	No
Project duration	Short	Long
Pirce of output	Predictable	Uncertain
Market for product	Rising	Uncertain
Competition in proposed market	Limited	Competitive
Political stability	Stable	Unstable
Expectations about ecomomy	Optimistic	Pessimistic
Sensitivity of project to shocks	Low	High
Spare capacity	Low	High

The Accelerator Principle

Investment activity in economies tends to be volatile, that is subject of considerable fluctuations. One of the explanations of this is the accelerator principle.

When demand for consumer goods and services is relatively stable in an economy, much of the demand for capital goods will take the form of replacing worn-out plant and machinery. However, if demand for final goods rises and there is no spare capacity in an industry, then new machinery will have to be purchased. Thus, the demand for capital goods will significantly increase to include new machines as well as replacement machines. Similarly, if the demand for final goods in an economy falls, firms will find they have over-capacity and too many machines. They will reduce the stock of machines to the new lower levels needed by not replacing worn out machines, so the demand for capital goods will fall. Thus, a rise in the demand for final goods will cause an accelerated rise in the demand for capital goods, and a fall in the demand for final goods will cause an accelerated fall in the demand for capital goods. The accelerator theory helps to explain the sudden fall in investment in 1990, in response to a fall in consumer demand.

Risk and Sensitivity Analysis

Sensitivity analysis is a technique for incorporating risk assessment in investment appraisal. It works by highlighting the key assumptions upon which investment appraisal figures were based. For example, revenue forecasts for an investment might be based upon:

- sales of 100000 units per year
- market growth of 3 per cent per year
- price of £3 per unit
- exchange rate of £1 = $1.5

Sensitivity analysis would calculate the effects on an investment appraisal of changes in these assumptions. Such analysis would demonstrate the effects of, example:

- sales of 80000 units per year
- market growth of 1 per cent per year
- price of £2.50 per unit
- exchange rate of £1 = $1.75

and thus illustrate a project's sensitivity to a variety of scenarios.

Sources of Funds

The main sources of funds for private sector investment include:

- retained profits
- new share issues
- loans
- government assistance

Government Policy

In general, right-wing governments interfere as little as possible in free markets, while left-wing governments are often prepared to offer financial assistance where a project provides employment in areas of high unemployment, or where there are wider community benefits. Exhibit 10.3 illustrates government funding for an urban-renewal project.

Exhibit 10.3: City Challenge: A Neat Stroke

City Challenge, the state-funded body responsible for urban renewal projects, has provided £195000 towards an eight-lane swimming pool that was opened in April at Spitalfields in Central London.

The 13-acre site, formely a fruit and vegetable market, was bought by developers who had planned a large housing and commercial complex but were blown of course by the recession.

The pool represents an interim use for the site which might otherwise remain derelict in a part of London with few local amenities and many social difficulties.

Source: The author, 1994

Review of Key Terms

- Investment = expenditure on capital goods and working capital.
- Fixed capital = durable capital goods such as buildings and machinery.
- Working capital = finance of work in progress such as raw material stocks, partially finished and unsold goods.
- Net investment = gross investment – depreciation.
- Payback method = appraisal technique to see how quickly an investment repays its costs.
- Average rate of return = appraisal technique where the average annual returns are expressed as a percentage of the original capital costs.
- Net present value = appraisal technique where all future revenues are recalculated to their present value so that a comparison can be made with the project costs.
- Internal rate of return = the rate of return of a project on capital employed, calculated by finding the rate that discounts future earnings to equal the capital costs.
- Accelerator theory = explanation why changes in consumer demand lead to larger changes in demand for investment goods.
- Sensitivity analysis = investigation of sensitivity of an investment project to changes in forecasts.

Data Questions

Task 10.1

Shares: Flights of Fantasy–Quentin Lumsden

One of the intriguing aspects of Euro Disneyland is that it is so difficult to value the shares. The stockbrokers SG Warburg has done projections, discounting back the stream of future earnings, to a figure from which it concludes the shares are fair value–and a hold–at the current 1650p. One number that stands out is the population of the catchment area for Euro Disneyland–some 400 million people. The projections on which many people have done their sums is that there will be 11 million visitors in the first year, rising gently thereafter. But if revenues grow more strongly than expected, the impact on profits will be dramatic because the costs are largely fixed. If there are 1 million more visitors than expected, or ticket prices in future years are 10 per cent higher than budgeted, or if visitors spend an extra pound more than expected on food and merchandise, then profitability will rise at a meteoric rate.

The reasonable conclusion is that Euro Disneyland has a considerable capacity to provide investors with favourable surprises.

Source: Independent on Sunday, 22 March, 1992 (adapted).

Will Mickey Turn his Back on Euro Flop?

The tragic tale of Euro Disneyland has dragged on since the Paris-based theme park opened its gates in April 1992. The fairy tale turned horror story is entering a new and crucial chapter. The figures are awesome; the park last year lost £607m. Euro Disney's share prices went into free fall following news of the losses last November and are currently trading around the 400p mark.

Source: Observer, 6 March, 1994 (adapted).

Questions

1. What is meant by 'discounting back the stream of future earnings'? Why is this done?
2. The first article was written just before the opening of Euro Disneyland. What factors would the writer have taken into account when evaluating Euro Disney's

potential profitability? Which of these factors were certainties?

3. What do the two articles demonstrate about investment appraisal?
4. Evaluate the Disneyland Paris (Euro Disneyland) investment project in the light of its performance to date.

Task 10.2: Reverberations from the Asian Economic Crisis

The domino effect of the slump in the Asian economies was demonstrated in 1998 by the sacking of 760 staff of Hong Kong's Cathay Pacific Airways. This represented about 5 per cent of its total workforce of 15000.

Speaking in 1998, David Turnbull, managing director of Cathay Pacific, said 'Just six months ago I would never have thought we would be forced to resort to such painful measures'. The cuts are the most dramatic in the history of Cathay pacific and follow a recent announcement to reduce the workforce in building maintenance and other services by 550. Mr. Turnbull underlined the urgency of the crisis by his comments on December 1997 figures for the airline which he described as 'truly appalling' when turnover fell by more than 25 per cent. The airline reported that 1997 had been a very bad year and that the prospects for 1998 showed few signs for improvement.

Other airlines operating in the region have been similarly affected. Philippine Airlines has an order for 15 new aircraft which were scheduled to be delivered in 1998–this contract has been put under review. The Australian airline Qantas, has reduced its services to Indonesia, Thailand and Malaysia. Similarly, Garuda, the state-owned airline of Indonesia has been unable to meet a payment for planes leased from Airbus.

The worry in Europe and America is that as airlines hit by the Asian economic crisis seek to reduce capacity this will have a severe knock-on effect leading to cuts in the production of aircraft–particularly by Boeing and Airbus. However, a spokesperson from British Aerospace was confident that a contract to supply 20 Hawk jets to Indonesia would survive the economic crisis.

Source: The author, 1999.

Questions

1. What is the accelerator principle? Explain its relevance and mechanism using this article.
2. What determines the demand of aircraft? Is this demand likely to be stable? How does the globalization of the economy affect the sales of aircraft?
3. The article suggests that 1998 would also be a difficult year for airlines. Supplementing your answer with more recent data if possible.

Task 10.3: City: Black Hole – Jeremy Warner

There was a depressing familiarity about last week's news that Eurotunnel has lost another round of its battle to keep the lid on the costs of the Channel Tunnel. Unless it can reverse the order on appeal, Eurotunnel is going to have to pay the Channel Tunnel contractors a lot more to complete the project than previously thought–making yet another refinancing of the venture look almost inevitable.

You don't need much experience of the construction industry to know that in all building projects the customer inevitably ends up paying considerably more than anticipated. At the risk of embarrassing Warburg Securities, however, I am going to quote from a City circular issued by the firm as part of the marketing effort for Eurotunnel shares when they were first sold to the public in the Autumn of 1987. 'We believe', the circular said, 'the balance of probability is that Eurotunnel will be completed both on time – May 1993 – and to budget.' The projected cost of the Channel Tunnel was then £4.8bn. After numerous upgradings, that figure had risen to more than £8bn by last November. It's a racing certainty that by the time the tunnel opens (late, naturally) the final tally is not going to be far south of £10bn – or roughly double the original estimate.

So were investors and bankers conned? Sir Alastair Morton, chief executive, and all the others involved in raising finance for Eurotunnel, no doubt were convinced that what they were saying was true. A part of this was to boast how the contracts had been deliberately designed to thwart the contractor's natural tendency to inflate his price. It's all proved so much hogwash and one suspects that deep down everyone must have guessed there wasn't a hope in hell of bringing the project in on budget. The imperative was to make sure it was built, a noble enough aim in itself, but hardly the first priority of the investor. It's possible the tunnel will still yield an adequate return, but it's looking increasingly less likely.

The inflated cost of the tunnel is only part of the problem. The greater imponderable is revenues once the system is up and running. It's hard to see why Eurotunnel's revenue predictions should be any more believable than its estimate of costs.

Source: Independent on Sunday, 5 April, 1992.

Questions

1. What would be an adequate return for the channel tunnel project? How would this be calculated?
2. Why are construction costs difficult to predict?
3. What impact does the late opening of the channel tunnel have on profit forecasts?
4. Why is this article sceptical about revenue predictions?
5. Evaluate the success of the Channel Tunnel.

Task 12.4: Port Aventura: Trying not to be a Black Hole

There are black holes and there are black holes. The one is a successful ride at Alton Towers. The other is the financial mess that EuroDisney got itself into. EuroDismal as named by its critics, now renamed Disneyland, Paris, down but not yet out.

The Disney fiasco seems perhaps a strange backdrop against which to launch Port Aventura, Europe's second biggest theme park, near Salou on the Mediterranean coast of Spain, due to open in April 1995.

In fact, the Tussauds group, owners of Alton Towers (and owned by Pearson, the *Financial Time*/Penguin books/Thames TV conglomerate), has been negotiating to become the theme park's largest shareholder and operating manager.

'Just because EuroDisney has got problems, it doesn't mean that major theme parks in Europe are bound to fail', says Ms. Rebecca Winnington-Ingram, a leisure industry analyst with

Morgan Stanley. And, of course, she is right. Perhaps, it is the success of Alton Towers in England that has tempted the Tussauds group into this £200m Spanish venture.

There are key differences between Port Adventura and EuroDisney, not least of which is the scale of the projects: Disneyland, Paris attracts 11 million visitors a year, but Port Aventura is forecasting 2.7 million in its first year rising to 6 million. Port Aventura is only open for 156 days a year under summer skies (when more than 15 million summer tourists are within easy reach), where Disneyland, Paris is open all year under much more threatening northerly skies.

Port Aventura has also avoided some of Disneyland, Paris's vast fixed costs by concentration on the theme park and not investing in the accommodation side. Ray Barret, a Tussauds director, offers the following analysis: 'EuroDisney got its theme park right and what went wrong was its inability to fill its [six] hotels.' The Mediterranean strip in which Port Aventura operates includes large resorts such as Benidorm and has an abundance of hotels already in existence.

The two parks also have a different gearing for their royalty, management and consultancy charges. The Walt Disney Corpoation took a massive 31.5 per cent of EuroDisney's operating income from its opening date. Similar charges payable from Port Aventura to Busch Entertainment (the park's designers) and to Tussauds (its managers) start at 12.4 per cent of operating income and are set to fall to 10.4 per cent by 1998.

Source: The author, adapted from press cuttings, January 1995.

Questions

1. Why is Port Aventura likely to be more of a successful investment project than EuroDisney?
2. Identify four key factors that might be used in conducting a sensitivity analysis on this investment and evaluate their possible impact.
3. Evaluate the success of Port Aventura.

11

INVESTMENT AND THE PUBLIC SECTOR

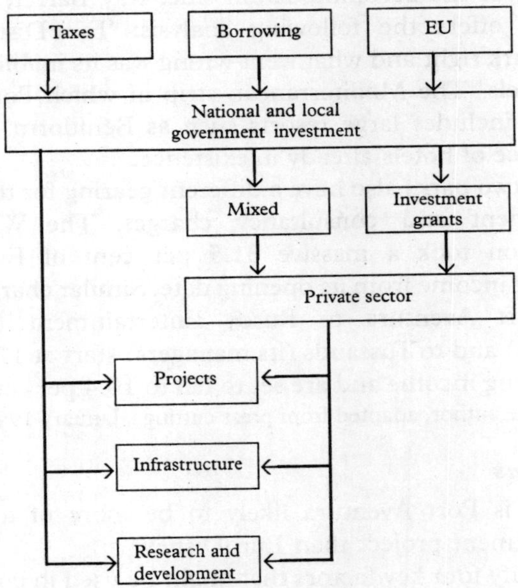

Objectives

The Thatcher revolution caused a fundamental rethink of publi investment in the UK as the government sought to 'roll back th frontiers of the state'. As of 1999, the Labour government ha maintained a similar stance. Opponents of public secto investment pointed to previous symbols of policy failure such as Concorde as representing the worst aspects of public sector investment–consuming ever-increasing sums of taxpayers' money and never achieving viable commercial sales. Thus, Mrs. Thatcher was adamant that the Channel Tunnel would be built using private funds or not at all. And so it was.

Yet the Channel Tunnel Project also demonstrates the shortcomings of such a policy. The French rail link has been upgraded using public funds, resulting in a fast, efficient journey from Paris to the tunnel at around 185 mph. However, Eurostar trains have to brake sharply to around 60 mph when they enter the British rail link to Waterloo. Lack of private or public funding has meant the track has not been upgraded, and is now unlikely to match the French link before the year 2005.

By studying this chapter students will be able to:

- identity the sources of public sector investment,
- identify different types of public sector investment,
- describe different methods of public sector investment,
- appraise public sector investment projects,
- identify public sector incentives for private sector investment,
- identify sources of funds for public sector investment.

Sources, Types, Methods and Aims of Public Sector Investment

Sources

Public sector investment can be financed from different sources. At the supranational level, the EU is a key source, particularly through the European Regional Development Funds. At the national level, government channels leisure and tourism investment through public corporations, quangos such as the Sports Council and government departments such as the Department of Culture, Media and Sport. Local government is the other major source of public sector investment.

Types

Public sector investment may also be classified according to type. First public sector investment may be in buildings and land, for example parks, leisure centres and museums. Second public sector investment includes plant and machinery such as playground apparatus, computerised booking systems and canal lock equipment. Third public sector investment may be made in infrastructure.

> **Exhibit 11.1: 'The Train Arriving at Runway 3...'**
>
> Passengers landing at Charles de Gaulle airport used to be faced by a messy onward journey into France. Now, a TGV high-speed station has been opened. The £300m glass and steel construction links four methods of transport: air, road, *metro* and high-speed rail. The TGV route is able to bypass Paris so that passengers can for example be in Lyons within 2 hours without having to change trains.
>
> Announced by the French government in 1987, the project was co-funded between French Railways (SNCF) and Aéroports do Paris (ADP). Further development of the site is to include banks, restaurants, shops and a Sheraton hotel.
>
> *Source:* The Author, from news cuttings, November 1994.

Infrastructure, or social overhead capital, is the construction needed to support economic development, for example, roads, railways and airports, water and sewerage, power and telecommunications. Public investment on infrastructure has been relatively higher in France than that in the UK and Exhibit 11.1 reports on the completion of a cornerstone in French public investment strategy.

Infrastructure development is a key part of tourism destination development as it has to precede specific project development such as hotels, leisure sites and restaurants.

Finally public sector investment may be spent on research and development, as illustrated in Exhibit 11.2.

Methods and Aims

The main methods of public sector investment are first *via* projects which are wholly public sector-financed, second *via* projects which are jointly financed by the public and private sectors and finally *via* projects which are private sector investments but which are eligible for public sector investment incentive grants.

Exhibit 11.2 Framework Programme 5: EU-funded Research and Development in the New Millennium

The fifth framework programme has a budget of Euros 15 billion and offers a strategic plan for the EU's research and development over a five-year period from 1999. Edith Cresson, the European Commissioner in charge of research and innovation, explained that the new programme is radically different form the previous one. 'We are moving from research based on performance for its own sake to resarch which focuses on the social and economic problems which face society today'.

The programme is divided into five thematic areas most of which include possible tourism and leisure. These are:

1. Quality of life and management of living resources.
2. User-friendly information society.
3. Competitive and sustainable growth.
4. Energy, environment and sustainable development.
5. Human potential and the socio-economic base.

R&D projects in leisure and tourism which have been funded by EU funds include

- ESCAPE—project to investigate pollution of coastal waters.
- A project to restore the stonework of European historic buildings by using laser techniques.
- TOURFOR—a project to use environmental management systems to limit environmental damage of tourism and recreation in forest areas.
- BRAIN—a project to develop mathematical models to improve soundproofing in aircraft cabins.

Source: The Author, from *RTD information.*

The aims of public sector investment include provision of goods and services which have significant public benefits, but which might not be profitable enough to attract private sector investment. Public sector investment may also be focused on projects aimed at the economic development or regeneration of a particular area. Exhibit 11.3 reports on the contribution of mixed public and private sector investment in the arts to the economy of Edinburgh.

Investment Appraisal in the Public Sector

Cost-benefit Analysis

Investment appraisal for private sector projects is relatively straightforward. If a project yields the required return on capital employed then the investment will go ahead.

Exhibit 11.3: Lights up for Edinburgh's New Theatre

In 1992 Lothian and Edinburgh Enterprise Limited—part of the Scottish Development Board—backed a £21 m project to turn a bingo hall into a theatre. It is a mixed investment where £6.6m has come from the private sector and no revenue subsidy will be needed in its operation. The result is a multi-use theatre with the largest stage in the UK.

The theatre represents a major project in Edinburgh's economic revival. It is estimated that 16000 extra tourists will be attracted to the city, boosting the city's tourism income by £7m to £257m.

Source: The Author, from news cuttings.

The different nature of the public sector makes investment appraisal more complex in this sector.

Some parts of the public sector are run on private sector lines. In these cases an investment is required to earn a specified rate of return on capital employed and thus the investment decision is fairly clear-cut.

However, many public sector investments are made for reasons of wider public benefits and thus private sector methods of appraisal are inappropriate. In such cases cost-benefit analysis provides a more useful method of project appraisal. All the costs and benefits of a project are identified and weighed up, including social as well as private ones.

Table 11.1

Cost-benefit Analysis of Canal Restoration Scheme

Costs	*Benefits*
Private costs	*Private benefits*
Construction costs of project, e.g.	Revenue from project, e.g.
• Materials	• Craft licences and charges
• Labour	• Fishing licences
• Professional fees	• Rentals from renovated buildings
Social costs	*Social benefits*
Inconvenience cost to local residents of construction	Drownings avoided through improved canal safety
	New jobs created by project
	Improved aesthetics of area

Table 11.1 shows an example of possible private and social costs and benefits for a canal restoration scheme.

Private sector investment appraisal of such a scheme would calculate the private costs of the project, and the private benefits. These would be discounted to net present value and since the private costs would almost certainly exceed the private benefits, the investment would not proceed.

However, cost-benefit analysis would analyse the wider costs and benefits. Some extra costs such as noise and congestion associated with the construction phase might be identified. Social benefits of the scheme would include lives saved through improved canal safety, greater public well-being caused by improved aesthetics from the project, and the effects on the local economy of new industries and employment attracted to the area because of the project. The total figures would be subjected to discounting to calculate net present value and it might well be the case that total public and private benefits would exceed costs. Thus, there may will be an argument for public sector investment in the project.

Other Factors Affecting Public Investment

Whilst cost-benefit analysis is used for appraising some major public sector investment projects, its use is far from widespread. Public sector investment decisions are often determined by the priorities of the political party in power at a national or local level. Decisions will also be affected by interest group activity, and the general economic environment. Public expenditure at a local level has come under increasing direct and indirect control from Central Government since 1979.

Task 11.2 of the data questions at the end of this chapter illustrates how a move to the left in the Labour party on Birmingham council led to a reversal of its public investment policy. 'City boosterism' had been the philosophy behind a massive investment in leisure, sports and arts facilities, designed to bring visitors and jobs to an area suffering from the effects of deindustrialisation. The new leadership has returned to a more conventional policy of investment in schools and housing.

Investment Incentives for Tourism and Leisure Projects

Areas of the UK which have high areas of unemployment are designated assisted areas, and the government uses incentives to attract firms and jobs to such areas. These include:

- *Regional selective assistance.* This is a discretionary grant based on the number of jobs that will be created and the capital costs of the project.
- *European Regional Development Fund.* This provides grants of up to 50 per cent for job-creating projects and projects to develop infrastructure.
- *Regional enterprise grants.* These encourage the growth of small businesses.

Exhibit 11.4 describes the steps taken by the European Commission to improve transport links in Europe, and the limited funding it has at its disposal.

Investment incentives are also available for some urban areas and are implemented through the following schemes:

- *Enteprise zones*–These small-designated areas of acute industrial decline have simplified planning rules and 100 per cent allowances against corporation tax for expenditure on buildings.
- *Urban development corporations*–These have considerable powers to clear and develop derelict sites and encourage private sector investment.
- *English partnerships*–This agency has inherited a large portfolio of factories, workshops and offices managed by English Estates.
- *City challenge*–This is a Department of the Environment initiative to encourage local authorities to bid for funds for projects to improve inner-city areas.

Finally, the Training and Enterprise Councils (TECs) can offer assistance in recuiting and training staff.

Exhibit 11.5 reports on public sector support for investment projects in leisure and tourism.

Exhibit 11.4: Trans-European Networks

Piece by piece, the transport system for Europe is dropping into place and 1998 saw the opening of Europe's longest suspension bridge, a 10-mile road and rail link between Denmark and Sweden. The link is part of a Euro 400 billion project called TENs or Trans-European Networks planned up to 2010.

But with EU funding for this network limited to Euros 5 billion between 1998 and 2003, the Transport Commissioner, Mr. Neil Kinnock, describes the role of the EU as one of pump priming, rather than full underwriter of costs. So EU expenditure is primarily targeted as feasibility and planning studies and securing funds from other sources.

These sources include the governments of EU member states and lenders such as the European Investment Bank and the European Investment Fund. Mr. Kinnock has also stressed a greater role for private sector funding, saying, 'we know that the conventional source of infrastructure investment–the public sector–is not going to be able to meet all the costs'.

By 2015 the TEN plan will improve rapid road and rail links across the EU and into the new member states of eastern Europe. The key TENs scheduled for completion by 2005 include:

- The Madrid-Barcelona-Montpellier high-speed rail link, connecting to the TGV network (Euros 16 billion).
- The Paris-Luxembourg-Strasbourg-Mannheim high-speed rail link (Euros 4.5 billion).
- The London-Paris-Brussels-Amsterdam-Cologne high-speed rail link (Euros 19 billion).
- The Greek motorway network (Euros 10 billion).

Source: The Author, 1999.

Exhibit 11.5: Leisure: Public Sector Investment Initiatives in 1999

The following examples shows support from a number of different public sector sources for leisure and tourism investment projects :

- Somerset District Council has opened a visitor centre on the River Parrett at Langport with financial help from the Rural Development Corporation.
- Tourism in Thanet has won funds from the European Regional Development Fund, and the UK Government Single Regeneration budget to support investment in local hotels and attractions.
- The Imperial War Museum is to build a 6000 square feet site in Manchester with a budget of £28.5 million. This is a mixed private sector/public sector initiative with £12.5 million coming from the private sector (Peel Holdings), £8.2 million from the European Regional Development Fund, and £2.5 million each from English Partnerships, Trafford Council and the Imperial War Museum.
- The Manchester Museum, the Manchester City Art Gallery and the Manchester Museum of Science and Industry share a £4.5 million grant from the European Regional Development Fund.

Source: The Author, 1999.

Sources of Funds

Sources of funds for public investment include.

- operating profits,
- taxation,
- borrowing,
- the national lottery.

Operating Profits, Taxation and Borrowing

Operating profits are rare in public sector organisations since they are run for motives other than profit. Thus, public sector investment is mainly financed from taxation receipts and government borrowing. This is a key reason why public sector investment is often under attack, particularly from the Treasury.

First opportunity costs are immediately apparent. Thus, the opportunity cost of more public investment is higher taxes, or less government expenditure elsewhere, as illustrated in Figure 11.1.

The circle represents total government spending and no increases in taxes or government borrowing are assumed. An increase in public sector investment from *A0B* to *A0C* can only be accommodated by a fall in other government expenditure of

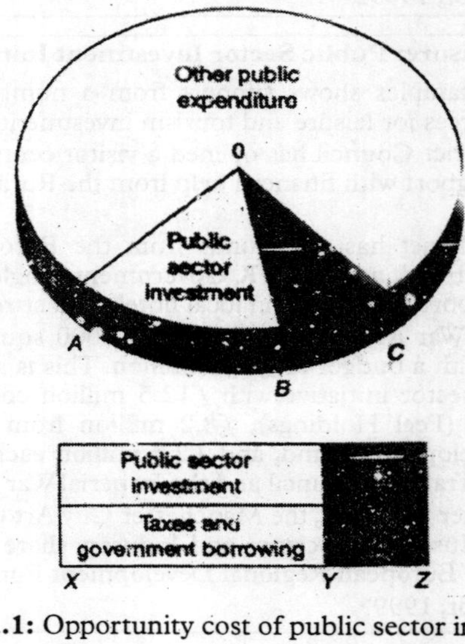

Figure 11.1: Opportunity cost of public sector investment.

BOC. Alternatively, it is assumed below that other government expenditure remains unchanged. In this case an increase in public sector investment from *XY* to *XZ* can only be financed through an increase in taxes or government borrowing of *YZ*.

Second, when the economy is performing badly, investment is often a target of government policy. If government borrowing is running too high, cutting social security payments or pensions has readily identifiable victims. Cutting investment generally results only in some improvement not taking place and therefore its consequences are more blurred.

The National Lottery

Whilst public spending is generally being squeezed by the Treasury, leisure and tourism is a key beneficiary of the National Lottery. Twenty-eight per cent of the lottery revenue (estimated at £5 billion annually 1998–2002) goes to five major causes, four of which will benefit leisure and tourism. These are charities, the arts, sports, national heritage and the Millennium Fund.

Projects in the arts which have benefited from the National Lottery include first, the South Bank arts complex in London. The National Theater has recently completed a major refurbishment of its foyer area with the help of lottery funds. Second, the lottery has provided investment funds for the Tate Gallery's proposed new Bankside museum for modern art. The estimated cost of conversion of a disused power station in east London for this project is estimated at £80m. The English National Opera is also seeking funds to renovate the London Coliseum.

The Sports Council has set up a lottery board to distribute its share of funds. Projects of between £5000 and £5m can be considered for a grant of up to 65 per cent. Large projects include a new national stadium and local council sports facilities.

The National Heritage memorial fund has responsibility for channelling funds into areas such as museum collections, historic buildings and monuments, landscapes, libraries and industrial heritage.

Other examples of contributions of lottery funding to leisure and tourism investment projects include the following which were announced in 1999:

- The Natural History Museum Earth Galleries (£6 million from Heritage Lottery Fund).
- National Trust renovation of Paul McCartney's Teenage Liverpool Home (£47500 from Heritage Lottery Fund).
- Redevelopment of Royal Naval Museum, Portsmouth (Heritage Lottery Fund).
- The National Space Science Centre, Leicester (£23 million from the Millennium Commission).

The Public Sector Investment Debate

Public investment has been subject to considerable debate during the Thatcher revolution and beyond. The Thatcher government took a stance against public investment based on the following arguments:

1. The public sector is not a good interpreter of people's wants and thus often invests in 'white elephants'.
2. The public sector is not good at ensuring efficient use of funds and tends to allow waste.
3. Public sector investment causes an increase in taxation or public borrowing.
4. Public sector investment 'crowds out' private sector investment.

The Thatcher government therefore removed a large slice of investment from the public sector through its privatisation programme. It then concentrated its efforts on creating an 'enterprise economy' which it hoped would stimulate private sector investment by reducing income and corporation tax and making the labour market more flexible.

The arguments favouring public sector investment are:

1. There is insufficient incentive for the private sector to invest in public goods.
2. The private sector underinvests in goods which have mainly social benefits.

Thus, where the market is used as the main determinant of investment, infrastructure projects with important public and merit angles will tend to be overlooked, despite the fact that the future capacity of the economy may depend on them. This has led to calls to distinguish between capital spending and current spending in PSBR figures, since the former will involve future benefits.

Review of Key Terms

- Infrastructure = construction needed to support economic development.
- Cost-benefit analysis = full analysis of public and private costs and benefits of project.
- New present value = discounting money paid at a future date to its present value.
- 'City boosterism' = investment in projects to regenerate city centres in economic decline.
- Assisted areas = areas of country eligible for government investment grants.
- Regional selective assistance = grant to attract job-creating projects.
- European Regional Development Fund = EU fund for projects and infrastructure to bring jobs to designated areas.
- Regional enterprise grants = grants to promote small businesses in assisted areas.
- Enterprise zones = designated areas of acute industrial decline having simplified planning rules and incentives expenditure on buildings.
- TECs = Training and Enterprise Councils.

Data Questions

Task 11.1: Canals and the Superhighway

No—its not that the UK's network of canals is about to take the oads off the roads. Its just a brilliant piece of lateral thinking hat is all part of British Waterway's (BW) search for additional evenue. The result—a creative fusion of the old and the new. Starting in Scotland, optical fibre cables are being laid along anal networks to meet the growing demand for data ommunications.

BW itself reflects an odd mixture of the old and new. At its centre is a network of partially derelict canals and navigable rivers, most of which are some 200 years old. But its chief executive, Mr. Brian Dice, brought with him modern management techniques honed over 25 years of working in the private sector at Cadbury Schweppes.

Private sector? But surely BW was itself privatised in the 1980s alongwith, amongst others, BT, BA and BAA. Apparently not. BW is still responsible to the Department of the Environment and privatisation was ruled out because of its continuing need for public subsidy.

But BW has not been immune to the harsh winds of economic reality and the Treasury has cut its annual funding over the past 10 years by around 25 per cent to an annual figure of £50m.

Brian Dice has sought to mitigate these cuts. 'I made it a priority that we stop whingeing and concentrate our efforts elsewhere, on the European Regional Development Fund, on Central Government's City Challenge and derelict land grant schemes and on local authorities and development corporations. The redevelopment of Sheffield canal basin, for example, uses all those sources. We are also keeping leisure fees for the 1 million boaters and anglers on our canals, marginally ahead of inflation. Freight traffic, principally on the navigable waterways of northern England, also enhances our revenues although no one is going to put computers on a barge. We have to exploit the honeyport sites and have more income under our own control. The transformation of Gloucester Docks, which now houses the National Waterways Museum, shows what can be done with local authority and private sector involvement. We are seeking similar partners for other undeveloped sites', he explains.

However, the Treasury prefers BW to sell of surplus sites for private sector development, rather than participate in joint ventures which might involve exposure to financial risk.

The canal network was overlooked for years, and despite recent renovations such as the Kennet—Avon canal in Wiltshire has a huge and urgent backlog of expensive repairs to lock gates leaking channels and aqueducts. Although it still carries some freight, its main future lies more as a source of recreation for boaters, anglers, walkers, cyclists and nature lovers. Nor should its conribution to the country's industrial heritage be overlooked.

But whilst people may agree on the importance of conservation and preservation is the current climate of environmental concern, the question as to how it is to be paid for remains unsolved.

Source: The author, from press cuttings.

Questions

1. What are the sources of investment funds for BW?
2. What sources of funds would be available to a privatised BW?
3. Compare the methods of determining the amount of investment in canals under private sector and public sector ownership.
4. Consider how the canal networks might appear by the year 2010, under private and public sector ownership.

Task 11.2: Rattled of Symphony Hall: Birmingham's bid for new greatness included balletic endeavour, Olympic attempts and brave new temples of culture. Then the city council changed its tune – Nick Cohen

When Simon Rattle raised his baton on 15th April, 1991 to lead the City of Birmingham Symphony Orchestra into the first chords of Stravinsky's *Firebird*, the idea that a funding crisis could bring the most acclaimed conductor in the country close to resigning would have seemed preposterous.

At the opening night of the Birmingham Symphony Hall the evidence of the city's bold, almost reckless commitment to economic regeneration through the spending of millions on culture, tourism and service industries could not have been more obvious to the 2200 guests. The symphony hall, everyone agreed, was one of the finest in the world. Labour-controlled Birmingham City Council had, with the support of local Conservatives, uncomplainingly paid the bulk of the £30m cost. No expense had been spared.

Next door, in Centenary Square, a £150m convention centre, which was confidently expected to attract business tourists from around the world, was all but complete. Behind the centre a new 13000-seat indoor athletics stadium which, city planners assured the voters, would help make Birmingham the UK sporting capital, was ready to receive athletes.

The policy of growth through prestige developments was outlined in a council development plan published shortly after the hall opened. 'To a large degree the prosperity of the whole city will depend on the city centre', it said. 'Entertainment, culture, leisure and recreation have an increasingly valuable role. Indeed, [they] represent the very essence of a large metropolitan international centre. In the seventies, the essence of Birmingham was making things people wanted to buy. But the recession of the early eighties wiped out 110000 jobs in a city of 1 million people. In desperation at first, then with an increasingly evangelical conviction, Birmingham's councillors turned to American models of urban regeneration pioneered in the rust-belt cities of Baltimore and Detroit. Civic boosterism is the jargon label—the belief that eye catching developments in the city centre could replace the lost manufacturing jobs by attracting high-spending tourists, conventioning businessmen and sports fans.

There were early warning signs that the policy was not working. Two Olympic bids failed in the eighties and a Super Prix car race collapsed. But it seemed almost bad taste at the time to mention these setbackes as the right-wing Labour council and their allies in business and the council bureaucracy exuberantly proclaimed that Birmingham 'was ready to compete with Barcelona and Lyon's.'

Birmingham's boosterism in the eighties has been followed by a profound shift in the city away form prestige projects to a kind of left-wing, back-to-basics policy. Last year, Theresa Stewart, a 63-year-old grandmother and veteran left-winger, beat the right-wing candidates for the Labour leadership on a policy of stopping the search for prestige. Ever since, there has been a changed atmosphere in the city. Education, housing, social services were the priority, not tourists, theatre-goers and conventions. 'For 10 years I was told the council was developing municipal socialism' she said after winning office. 'It's been more like municipal stupidity.' Ed Smith, the orchestra's general manager, recognises the shift in emphasis. 'Not a day goes by without money worries,' he said. Other attractions are also in trouble.

Councillor Stewart has said she would 'not sped £10 on another Olympic bid'

Stand outside the gleaming concert hall and strike out in any direction and in 15 minutes you will hit Birmingham's inner city—a ring of misery running clockwise from Handsworth through New Town, Aston, Small Heath and Sparkbrook to Ladywood. The statistics give a prosaic idea of the poverty. In the nine inner-Birmingham wards, 31 per cent of adults are out of work. Almost four out of 10 of the city's population receive state benefits. In the New Town district, to take just one example, the number of single-parent families is three times the national average and two out of three residents do not have a single O-level or GCSE. If the symphony hall, convention centre and the rest were really to be the source of regeneration, then these are the people who should have benefited from the trickle-down effect. They have not. Most of the jobs created were menial, part-time and low-paid. The council recognised the problem and devised a training programme to prepare the unemployed for full-time work in the convention centre. The result was pitiable. Just 19 inner-city residents got jobs. More significantly, money was diverted from the core services the poor depend on to fund the building boom. An analysis by the University of Central England (formerly Birmingham Polytechnic) estimated that £123m was taken from Birmingham City Council's housing budget and that spending on school buildings fell by 60 per cent while the lavish city centre developments were being built. Most notoriously of all, the council took more and more from the budget for education, leaving Birmingham with some of the worst schools in the country. In 1991 Birmingham was spending £46m less than the amount recommended by Central Government. Birmingham city centre may look marvellous, but it is a gleaming heart

surrounded by a decaving body Councillor Stewart cannot knock down the convention centre, much as she may like to, and the symphony hall and indoor arena will remain. But it is clear that from now on the council's priorities will be housing and education. An extra £43m will be pumped into schools this year and the money will have to come from somewhere.
Source: *The Independent*, 9 March, 1994 (adapted).

Questions

1. What was the economic rational behind 'city boosterism'?
2. What factors would you take into account in conducting a cost-benefit analysis on investment in 'city boosterism'?
3. What factors caused a change in Birmingham's investment strategy?
4. What were the opportunity costs of 'city boosterism;' in Birmingham?

Task 11.3: Public Spaces: Lost Victorian Heritage

1832: The Whig government conceives the idea of 'public walks'.

1837: Joseph Hume MP tables a parliamentary motion calling for the provision of open spaces to be financed from the public purse for the enjoyment of the public.

1840: The Arboretum in Rosehill, Derby, is opened to fanfares and tireworks. Joseph Strutt commends the park as offering local workers 'the opportunity of enjoying, with their families, exercise and recreation in the fresh air and in public walks and grounds'. The Arboretum is planted with 913 types of trees and shrubs and more than 1000 types of rose.

1979: Mrs. Thatcher comes to power. Public sector spending cut.

1998: Patrick Weir of the *Guardian* surveys the sorry state of the park. He reports: 'The Lodge House, at the Rosehill Street entrance, serves bleak notice of what lies beyond: a crumbling, boarded up edifice, it would look more at home on a Hammer Horror set. Once in the park, signs of decay are all too evident. Public monuments are in disrepair, the bandstand in burned down, statues are missing and the centrepiece fountain is fenced off. Trees remain untrimmed, while graffiti, litter and dog dirt scar the environment. Gangs congregating at night render the park even less inviting'.

1999: Derby City Council awaits the result of a bid to the Heritage Lottery for £3 millions. The council has made provision to access an initial £200000 of lottery funds by providing £43000 in matched funds, but it is not confident of finding the next tranche of £750000 necessary to release the rest of the lottery's £3 millions.

Steve Jardine, of the DERBYES! Campaign, hopes that residents, local businesses and grant-providing trusts can help. He said: 'The council can't do everything. People must be more proactive. It's a case of priorities and how much we value our parks. They are the lungs of the city, and, as recognized by the Victorians, areas where people can relax and play.'

Source: The author based on article in the *Guardian*.

Questions

1. What differing government attitudes to public sector investment does this article demonstrate?
2. What are the arguments for and against leaving provision of parks and gardens to the private sector?
3. Given the shortage of local council funds–suggest ways in which improvements in this park could be financed.
4. Explain the meaning of the terms *opportunity cost*, *crowding out*, *merit goods* and *public goods* in relation to this article.

Task 11.4: Three Trains and a Bridge

Railtrack, UK: Railtrack, the privatised owner of the UK rail infrastructure, announced in 1998 plans to spend £17 billion over the next decade on investment in the railways. Sir Robert Horton, Railtrack's chairman described Railtrack's plan as 'a blueprint to regenerate the railways.'

However, other commentators saw the proposed investment in a different light. The rail regulator Mr. Jobn Swift criticised Railtrack for a failure to invest adequately in the industry and announced he would be carrying out a detailed investigation into the sufficiency of Railtrack's plan. He said of Railtrack: 'Its statement contains very few commitments to deliver significant improvements across the rail network which passengers can recognise. I therefore intend to find out from train operators and funders of the railway whether Railtrack's statement meets their reasonable needs as required by its licence. I must be satisfied the Railtrack has sought to identify these requirements and reflect them in practical plans to improve the railway'.

Mr. David Bertram, chairman of the central rail users' consultative committee, added to the criticisms saying: 'We had hoped for something more ambitious. The £4 million a day due to be spent by Railtrack may well not be sufficient, and the easing of congestion at many key points is only at the planning stage, with no firm dates yet'.

The London Underground, UK—The London Underground is to remain in public ownership but will receive a substantial injection of private finance. It is to benefit from a £7 billion programme of private-sector investment to be carried out over 15 years. Future plans for the Underground had included privatisation but the government has opted for a private-public partnership.

Skye Bridge, UK—Sye bridge spans the sea between the Isle of Skye and the Scottish mainland and was built under the private finance initiative (PFI). Under this programme public schemes are funded by private money. A private sector consortia designed, built and financed the bridge, and shouldered risks such as construction delays. In return the government entered into a contract to pay for yearly use of the bridge.

The Madrid—Seville High-speed Train, Spain—The Spanish Ministry of Transport paid for the pts 450 bn construction costs of the high speed train from Madrid to Seville which opened in 1992. It has been such a success that it later authorised the construction of the extension from Madrid to the French frontier to link with the TVE system. This should be completed by 2003.

Source: The author, 1999.

Questions

1. What different types of investment are demonstrated in this article?
2. In each case what is the main determinate of the level of investment?
3. What are the benefits and drawbacks of investment in transport schemes under regimes of:
   - Private sector
   - Private/public sector partnerships
   - Public sector?
4. What factors would be taken into account in a cost-benefit analysis of the Madrid-Seville high-speed train?

12

THE TECHNOLOGICAL ENVIRONMENT AND OPPORTUNITIES

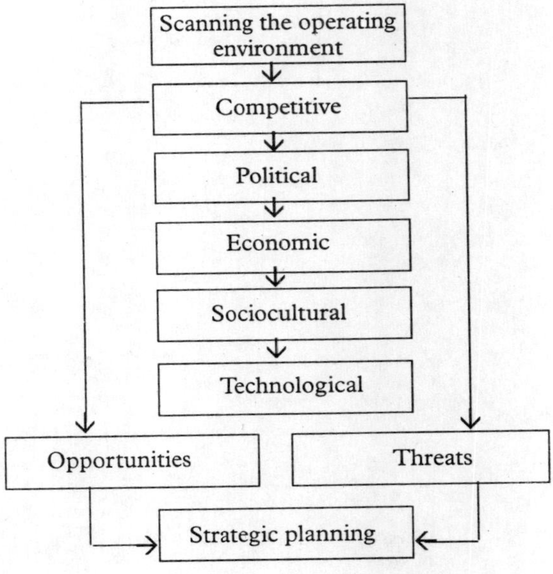

Objectives

First, this chapter concludes PEST analysis by considering the extent and impact of the continuing technological revolution.

Second, this chapter introduces the concept of opportunities and threats analysis. It provides a useful tool for organisations to identify the key changes in their operating environment and thus acts as a sound basis for reviewing the appropriateness of the organisation's strategy.

By studying this chapter students should be able to:

- Define the scope of the technological environment.
- Identify information sources for analysing the technological environment.
- Identify technological opportunities and threats to leisure and tourism organizations.
- Conduct an audit of an organisation's operating environment.
- Conduct an opportunities and threats analysis.

The Technological Environment

Technological change offers two key opportunities for leisure and tourism organisations. First it can lead to cost reductions. The long-run average cost curve (LRAC) is constructed on the assumption that technology remains constant, and thus improved production technology will cause the long-run average cost curve of an organisation to fall, as illustrated in Figure 12.1 LRAC1 represents the original long-run average cost curve. The use of improved production technology enables the curve to shift downwards to LRAC2. Average costs of producing level of output 0C now fall from *0*A to *0*B.

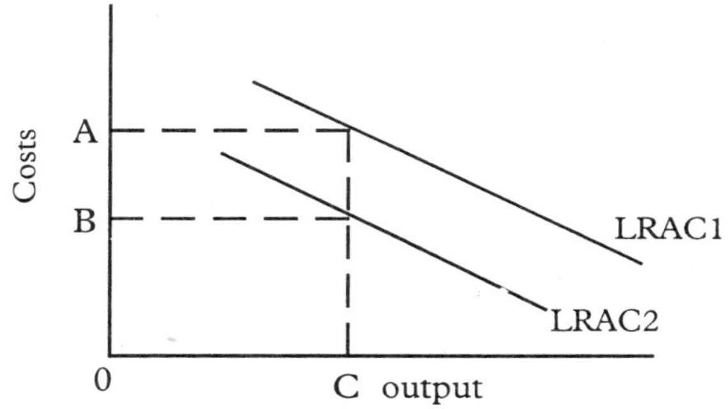

Figure 12.1: Shifting long-run average cost curve (LRAC).

Second, technology can provide new products and markets. Both of these routes can lead to an improvement in an organisation's competitive edge, and can be the basis of price-based or differentiation strategies. However, technological change also poses threats where existing products become obsolete in the face of new developments. Technological change is being delivered mainly at present by the increased processing power of micro-computers, the provision of high capacity datalinks and the fall in price of hardware and software. Silicon chip developments lead to faster data processing. Fibre optics and digital technology mean that data can be quickly transmitted globally at low cost, and these hardware developments mean that software of ever-increasing sophistication can be developed.

Multimedia is one of the key developments of the 1990s. It is illustrated in Figure 12.2.

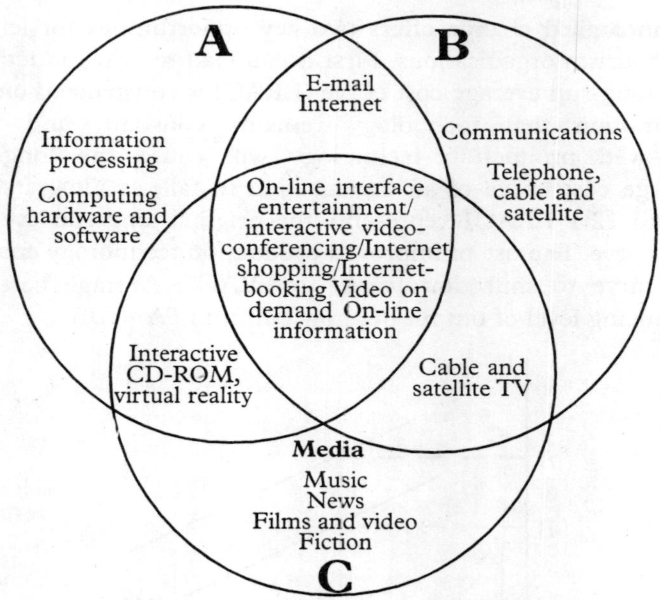

Figure 12.2: Multimedia.

Thus, at a simple level an organisations's computer network on its own can perform word processing, accounting and other functions (circle A). Linked to other computers *via* datalink services it can access reservation systems and provide E-mail and Internet conferencing (circles A+B). Linked to other media, at the simplest level text, images and video clips can be incorporated into software programmes (circles A + C). At the most sophisticated level virtual reality can be set up. Linking PCs and media sources through datalinks provides access to the whole repertoire of computer applications (circles A + B + C). This includes, for example, video on demand, and Internet shopping which enables goods to be chosen at home and delivered to your door. Home-booking allows access to central reservation and booking systems from home, with the possiblility of video clips of resorts and hotels.

Exhibit 12.1 describes how computer technology is paving the way to ticketless travel.

Technological impacts may be analysed in the following areas:

- hospitality
- tourism
- leisure

Hospitality

Showcases such as Hotech, the exhibition for suppliers of hotel technology, provide a good insight into innovations affecting the hospitality industry. Current developments include the following.

First links into central reservation systems are important so that hotels can capture reservations generated from distant terminals. Most travel agents use one of the central reservation systems such as SABRE or Amadeus to book air travel, car hire and accommodation and access to these systems represent an important marketing tool. For the future, a system that automatically rebooks accommodation to deal with air delays and missed connections is a possibility.

Second, there has been considerable progress in accounting packages. In management accounting, yield management packages are an important tool enabling hotels to maximise revenue by adjusting rates to best-fit changing market conditions. Yield management packages are able to compare likely demand with actual demand and capacity and suggest

Exhibit 12.1: No More 'Tickets Please'

Almost 50 per cent of passengers flying in the USA now fly ticketless. Travel agents and airlines can book a passenger on to a flight using electronic ticketing without issuing a physical ticket. When a passenger books a flight all that happens is that a reservation is made in the airline's computer system. The system can save large sums in airlines costs and helps passengers too. Passengers identify themselves at check-in by their passport or credit card.

United Airlines is at the forefront of ticketless travel development, whilst Lufthansa leads the way in Europe and Cathay pacific in the Far East. However, the system does have its critics and a United spokesperson admitted that some travel agents were worried about computer ticketing in case business was lost as passengers cut out the agent and booked direct with the airline. But he added, 'Agents will find their paperwork greatly reduced, and that they save a lot of money by not having to bike or express-post tickets to customers'.

Meanwhile, British Airways is developing Internet booking and its website allows passengers in over 50 countries to book and pay for tickets anywhere on the airline's network. BA's head of global distribution, Roger Flynn, looks to future development which will involve smart cards and palm or iris-reading identification machines.

BA has also introduced automatic ticket machines at its major airports. These allow passengers to use a credit card to buy a ticket at a machine where they use a touchscreen to select a seat. A boarding pass is printed out in under a minute.

Source: The Author.

rates accordingly. In financial accounting, packages enable financial reporting to take place speedily and efficiently.

Check-in time can be minimised by using credit card readers to automate registration and issue a high-technology key which can even be a creadit card itself. High-technology keys reduce the possibility of theft since codes may be changed frequently at minimal cost. It is possible for a reservation system to use its database to provide personalised services such as provision of a particular newspaper. Computerised reservation systems can also reduce check-out time to a minimum.

Other computer-assisted management systems range from energy management systems to conference management systems and computer-intelligent buildings. A computer-intelligent building means that most of the functions of the building are computer-assisted, and so, for example, room cleaning schedules can be computer-generated from information from guests' smart keys, pay rolling can be generated from reading employees' time sheets which themselves are based on electronic monitoring, and a wide range of on-screen services are available in rooms.

Exhibit 12.2 shows how technology has been used to cut costs, enabling some French hotels to pursue an effective price-based strategy.

The conference industry illustrates possible opportunities and threats posed by new technology. A recent study found that 36 per cent of hotel room sales was made to conference delegates, and there has been growth in the number of centres

Exhibit 12.2: Hi-tech Hotels are Revolutionizing Budget Accommodation in France—Rob Davidson

You're driving through France and decide to stop for the night. The question is: how do you break your journey without breaking the bank? The answer is the budget hotel where a clean, quiet room for up to three people sharing costs from £15 a night.

How are overheads kept so low? Most cost-trimming is achieved by reducing services to a bare minimum. Hi-tech, manpower-saving devices also help to cut costs. A good example is automatic check-ins, which are placed at entrances for use when reception areas are unattended. *La Réception Automatique* works like a cash machine: you insert a credit card and 'converse' with the facility (in French, English or German) about the room you want, how long you plan to stay and whether you want breakfast. The machine then debits your card and issues a key and room number.

French technology is also applied in the automatic cleaning systems installed in the showers and lavatories of the hotels. Every time the facility is used, a powerful spray of a water-disinfectant mix ensures that it is left spotless for the next user.

The labour-saving devices and basic services mean that budget hotels can be run by just two people plus cleaning staff.

Source: The Independent.

with capacities for in excess of 1000 delegates. However, firms such as Xerox are increasingly turning to video-conferencing as a way of reducing travel and hospitality costs, and saving expensive executive time. Some hotels are responding to this challenge and the Hilton National group for example has introduced video-conferencing in its key conference venues.

However, with the growth of multimedia technologies it is possible that more conferencing will in future be office-or home-based, utilising PCs. It is possible to access video clips of speakers *via* point-and-click menus and organise discussion

Exhibit 12.3: The Future is Virtually Here–David Bowen

It is 2008 and you are going into a meeting with your bosses. They are in San Francisco and Bavaria; you are in your house in the Scottish Highlands. You sit down in your office, put on a pair of dark glasses and a glove–both linked by wire to the computer on your desk. You find yourself in an electronic 'room', with a table and chairs. You look round to see your American boss–or rather his hologram–sitting next to you. A moment later the German appears, and the meeting starts. Using your glove you can pass electronic documents around the room–a disembodied hand appears in front of you, to mimic your movements. This is a virtual conference.

In the multimedia world, we are told, we will be able to shop, play, learn and even make love while sitting alone in the house. The virtual conference is a three-dimensional (3D) computer graphic, transmitted by telephone. Combined with 3D spectacles it tricks the brain into believing that it is inside an electronically created room.

Computers sufficiently powerful to digitalise have become available. A CD can store the equivalent of two digitalise editions of the *Encyclopaedia Britannica.* So all we need is the 'information superhighway', a telephone line with the capacity to carry all this information. The present copper phone wire can carry only voice and a limited amount of text and data. Replace it with fibreoptic cable and its capacity increases 250000 times over. The entire contents of Oxford's Bodleian Library could be transmitted in 42 seconds.

Source: Independent on Sunday.

groups with video or e-mail links. Similarly, questions can be collected over the conference period and feedback made available on menus. Conferencing has become more flexible and personalised as participants can choose speakers, discussion groups and questions of direct relevance to themselves, and indeed can browse and move between areas with ease. The implications of such a move would be a shift in conference spending away from airlines, hotels, and local hospitality providers towards the providers of datalinks and other hardware and software companies. Exhibit 12.3 describes a possible video-conference of the future.

Travel and Tourism

Technological changes in transportation are likely to be extensions of existing technologies in the form of larger jumbo jets, and faster trains for travel. Additionally some shortages of air space may be relieved by using information technology to create smaller air tunnels than the existing air corridors.

Booking and reservation systems are likely to become more sophisticated, globalised and more widely available. The main distribution channels currently are Worldspan, SABRE, Amadeus and Galileo and there have been some disputes between the systems providers and the service providers over charges.

The early entry of American Airlines into computerised reservation systems has given it a competitive advantage in its SABRE system which now generates more profits than the airline operations. Multimedia is filtering into computerised reservation systems and SABREVISION now adds pictures and video images of destinations to information about price and availability.

The increasing use of the Internet may pose some threats to travel agents. Use of NetScape Navigator and Internet Explorer to access the web makes home use straightforward and SABRE is now available *via* the Compuserve network to home-based PCs. The Windows environment means that it can be used instantly, whereas travel agents had to undergo a half-day training to use the pre-Windows system.

Exhibit 12.4 records that the impact of the Internet on booking services had grown substantially between 1994 and 1999.

Leisure

The multimedia revolution offers the prospect of sophisticated home-based leisure and enhancement of attractions away from home.

Exhibit 12.4: Internet Travel on-line for Expansion

In 1994 under the heading 'Computers: meagre catch on the travel lines', the *Independent* newspaper reviewed the impacts of PCs on travel bookings. It quoted one travel expert who commented 'On-line services are great tools for finding schedules and fares but they usually lack the ability to book the absolutely last available seat on a plane.' It found a limited market and conclude that 'A bargain fortnight in Benidorm courtesy of the home computer is probably still a few years away'.

By 1999 things had changed considerably. The Internet was well established, both physically and in the mind of suppliers and consumers. Connections were faster and navigation tools better. As more households become connected to the Internet, so it is becoming a more important source for travel bookings and information. For example, travel guides are available on the net. The Lonely Planet website (www.lonelyplanet.com) reported over 63 million hits per month in January 1999. As well as providing standard information, it also posts recent feedback on destinations. Rob Flyn, the site manager said, 'The site is becoming like a daily paper offering today's news for tomorrow's traveller'. Destinations also run their own websites providing details for sightseeing and links with accommodation and restaurants.

Yellow pages (www.yell.co.uk) has a travel facility which offers flights, accommodation, car hire and holidays. One of its key attractions is the posting of around 75000 late deals which are updated every 30 minutes. The site started s a travel information facility and developed into an on-line booking service. One part of its offering is an airline ticket auction. This is a system that posts last-minute airline tickets on the web and invites bids from potential customers, with the tickets being allocated to the highest bidders.

On-line travel booking offers costs savings to suppliers and information benefits to consumers. Consumers also get quicker access to booking on a well-designed site and can avoid long waits on hold that characterise some telephone booking services. suppliers are keen to move towards more Internet bookings and Delta Air Lines introduced a $2 surcharge on non-internet bookings. However, it abandoned this after criticism from US travel agents (1999). EasyJet, the UK budget airline offers a £1 reduction each way on seats booked *via* its website (www.easyJet.com).

Booking sophisticated tourism services such as holidays may continue to provide a future for traditional travel agents who have specialised training and can put together complex itineraries. But for straightforward services such as airline seats, hotel reservations, and seats for major entertainment, on-line booking is likely to make substantial inroads into the high street agents business in the foreseeable future.

Source: The Author, 1999.

Exhibit 12.5: Sex Comes on-line

1994: *Virtual Valerie* was the cutting edge of technology for porn–a CD ROM game where 'Val obeys the user's every command.'

1999: Karlin Lillington of the *Guardian* gives and update on the technological progress of porn: 'Not even the defence industry capitalises on new technical developments as swiftly, and with as much innovation and payback, as the pornographers. They buy the best equipment, use some of the best Internet service companies in the business to give them ultra-fast connections directly to the Internet's backbone, and are always eager to test the newest applications—anything to push images as fast as possible to the paying punters at the end of the mouse. From web video to live chat, on-line credit card transactions to image compression technologies, the on-line sex industry usually got there first and pioneered the format. As a result, the Internet has made silicone as ubiquitous as silicon. Sex is the web's killer application.

An IT applications engineer notes that pornography is one of the key industries involved in the purchase of computer equipment. The economics of porn provide the motive for state-of-the-art expertise to provide competitive advantage. A third of web users surveyed reported that they had accessed a sex site. These billions of hits generate subscriptions and sales. For example, a Los Angeles-based website called Danni's Hard Drive had a gross turnover of $2.7 million in 1997 rising to around $3.5 million in 1998. The site averages 5 million hits a day and has established a client base of over 22000 paying subscribers. Access costs $14.95 per month which gains entry to photos, videos and six live real-time acts.

Industry analysts Forrester Research estimate that pornography produced $.137 million for US websites in 1997, and $185 million in 1998. Forrester predicts that by 2001 revenue will have risen to $366 million. This makes pornography third in Internet sales after computers and travel. *Inter@ctive,* a magazine for the web industry, estimates that the supply of adult sites for 1997 was about 10000.

The Hot & Heavy site boasts 'the hottest 3D virtual reality sex online', and entices its customers to 'use your' mouse to move the hottest girls/couples in 3D.' But what of the future?

2002: Programmers predict that cybersex will take on new dimensions with developments in 'teledildonics'. Here cybersex moves from visual interaction nearer to virtual sex where visual interaction is merged with sensation.

2008: One cybersex futurologist predicts 'the ability to get and give virtual satisfaction through sensory interactivity'. This would involve donning a helmet to ente a virtual world and a suit to receive and transmits touch sensations. In fact, a German research group have already produced a prototype of a full-body sensory suit for virtual sex.

Source: The Author, 1999.

In the home, video on demand may spell the demise of the video rental store. Digitised movies will be stored in distant databases which can be accessed *via* a menu and decoding system using cable.

Interactive games which started life on floppy disks are able to exploit the extra speed and memory of CD-ROM technology. Exhibit 12.5 illustrates the development of interactive porn.

Currently, the ultimate development goal of computer games appears to be virtual reality. Virtual reality, or cyberspace as it is sometimes called, is an extension of the technology of the flight simulator. It enables participants to enter a computer-generated three-dimensional environment and interact with the environment. Headsets, data gloves and data suits are the passport to this cyberworld where participants can travel from scene to scene and interact with cyber people and cyber objects.

Exhibit 12.6: Three Hedgehogs Pay Out?

Kunick, the leisure operator reported pre-tax profits for the half-year to the end of March 1998 of £4.8 million. This represented an 11.5 per cent rise over the same period for 1997.

Kunick is a supplier and operator of fruit machines and part of its development strategy has been to upgrade this product to reflect changes in technology. To do this it has entered into a joint venture with Sega. The idea is to capture Sega's experience in high-tech and Internet amusement products and breathe a new lease of life into a product which has undergone little change.

The new machines will be networked to a central computer. They will include a range of different amusements which the user can select from an on-screen menu. Russell Smith, chief executive of Kunick, explains: 'They will be multiple-game machines. They will also be easier to upate – we will be able to introduce new twists'. The new machines also offer benefits from the point of view of maintenance since thay can be monitored for faults by the central computer.

Source: The Author, 1999.

Virtual reality is also likely to affect leisure away from home. Sega has developed theme parks in Japan with interactive attractions which will let people shoot and steer their way through adventures. Disney utilises virtual reality in its heritage theme park in Washington DC so that visitors can experience life as a civil war soldier, or as a slave. The future interpretation of heritage may well rely less on exhibits in glass cases and more on participation and interaction with virtual artefacts and virtual historical figures. Exhibit 12.6 explores the world of virtual theatre.

Opportunities and Threats Analysis

An opportunities and thereats analysis examines an organisation's operating environment. The operating environment can be audited using the framework and this is illustrated in Table 12.1.

Once the key opportunities and threats have been established for an organisation, its strategic plan can be updated to show how opportunities can be exploited and threats can be countered. Table 12.2 considers the main opportunities and threats facing BA in 1994.

Review of Key Terms

- Fibreoptics = high-capacity data transmission lines using optical fibre rather than copper wire.
- CRS = computerised reservation system, such as SABRE or Amadeus.
- Multimedia = combination of media sources (e.g. video), computing and communications.
- Computer-intelligent building = building use monitored and controlled by computer (e.g. security, temperature, staff location, room use).
- Digitalisation = transforming images and sound to digital code for ease of storage and transmission.
- NetScape Navigator and Internet Explorer = Windows-based operating systems for Internet use.
- Internet provider = company which provides Internet access to PC user.
- Networked computers = computers linked to other computers.
- Interactive = user response encouraged and allowed.
- Virtual reality = computer-generated three-dimensional environment for user interaction.
- Cyberspace = virtual reality environment.

Table 12.1
Opportunities and Threats Analysis

Environment	*Opportunities*	*Threats*
Competitive		
Threat of entrants		
Power of buyers		
Power of suppliers		
Threat of substitutes		
Competitive rivalry		
PEST		
Political		
Economic		
Sociocultural		
Technological		

Table 12.2
Opportunities and Threats Analysis for British Airways 2000

Environment	*Opportunities*	*Threats*
Competitive		
Threat of entrants	• Limited slots available at Heathrow • Introduction of 'GO' – own no-frills airline	• Debonair, Ryanair, easyJet • Competition from other European gateways.
Power of buyers		• Overcapacity on transatlantic routes
Power of suppliers		• BAA monopoly of main UK airports • Limited competition between aircraft and engine manufacturers • Costs of non-BA CRS
Threat of substitutes	• Poor performance of UK rail companies Road congestion	• TGV in Europe • Eurostar routes to Paris and Brussels
PEST		
Political	• EC rules forbidding subsidies to airlines of member states	• Monopoly investigations into mergess and alliances • Environmental lobby against pollution

Environment	*Opportunities*	*Threats*
		• Continuing uncertainty over extra terminal at Heathrow
Economic	• Currency fluctuations	• Currency fluctuations
	• Robust domestic, EU and US economies • Low costs of aviation fuel	• Recession in Japan, Economic difficulties in Asia, South America and Russia • Taxes on air travel
Sociocultural	• Move towards multiple holidays each year	
Technological	• Larger aircraft • On-line booking • Improved yield management systems	• Overcrowding of airspace • Millenniumbug

Data Questions

Task 12.1: Segaworld, London—Queue: What a Torture, by John Tribe

'Welcome to the next generation of futuractive theme parks', and what better place for an indoor park than in the middle of a city which is wet and cold for at least half of the year. *We 'take the rocket escalator to another dimension*, and it feels good–the steep, long escalator ride to the apex of the Trocadero centre excites the senses. We are on the threshold of *'a galaxy of futuristic experiences in one world'*.

Breathless with anticipation we are delivered into what must be the first themed area—'Receptionland'. Our first encounter with *Segapeople* is with a man who wants to take our photo. Hmm, we dodge round him, puzzle about what to do, where to go. This *futuristic* world is strangely signless. But look–the queue has not been abolished in this brave new world–and an ordinary kind of sign says its going to be 45 minutes. This must be the place to start.

The kids–there are twelve of them in our party–just cannot wait to encounter the 'Beast in Darkness'. They push and crane their necks round every corner. Eventually we reach its 'lair'. Well it's dark but I must say not terribly beastly. We just wander found corridors, regaled by the occasional roar through some speakers and pass a few video screens showing a *beast* going about its daily routines. Then–oh dear, this is so scary–the floor becomes *uneven. Oooh! Aaah!* Funnily enough the next bit had us all leap out of our skins–a *Segaperson* jumped out on us from around a corner. An old trick, but a good one (and what turned out to be the most exciting moment of the day).

He put us on a ride. Now the kids were scared again. Where were they going? They fought to be with an adult. As our cart set off I recalled my first themepark experience–The Black Hole at Disneyland, California, some 20 years ago. When that cart shot off into the dark, I could only scream out involuntary oaths as it hurtled round its impossible track. It was pure sensation, exhilaration and entertainment.

But the cart in *the beast's lair* just trundled. The commentary said something like '*the beast has escaped its going to get you*'. I felt oddly safe ... but I hadn't figured on the special effects. The back of my seat took on a life of its own. Almost as if a *beast was trying to get at me.* But my sweatglands were not activated, my pulse missed not a beat, my adrenaline pump failed to kick in. Matthew, aged 8¾, yawned. And that was *The Beast in Darkness.*

Points

Futuricity: 1970s
Beastliness 1/10
Pulse rate: 72 beats per minute
Screamometer: 0 decibels

We skirted *The Combat Zone,* an arcade full of slot machines and arrived at our next queue for *Aqua Planet. Aqua Planet* was worth the 45-minute wait. We were strapped into seats, and plunged headlong into a breathless journey. It was virtually real. Things jumped out from the screen, we ducked instinctively to avoid collisions. The illusion worked. It was old technology–3D plastic specs, and tilting seats–but as the brochure brags '*try telling your brain it's not real*'.

Points

Excitement: 7/10
Fun: 8/10

We pass another hanger of slot machines–*Race Track*–down a floor to *Space Mission*. Unfortunately, it's *mission impossible* due to maintenance problems.

Points

Length of kid's faces: very long
Robustness of Ride: 0/10 (it is only 5 weeks old)

Just in case you're getting slot machine withdrawal symptoms another huge suite looms into view–*Flight Deck.*

Down another level – we try to join the queue for *Ghost Hunt*. It's just malfunctioned so we have to wait 5 minutes to join the queue. The queue, once reached is long, hot, boring and slow moving. You '*try telling your brain it's not's not* real' but this is no virtual queue. Over and above the malfunction, *Ghost Hunt* has technical problems. It's only working at half capacity. Still a *Segaperson* hands out free tickets to our kids to make up for the wait. Nice touch I think. What can they do with them? '*They can redeem them at the concession–you need 25 points minimum for a SegaPencil.*' The kids count their tickets–they have 10 each.

Ghost Hunt is bizarre. You get in another cart on another train. You trundle round. Targets appear in front of you. You try to shoot them down. Its just like a regular amusement arcade machine, only its put on a cart. Weird.

Points

What was the point?

We spill out of '*Ghost Hunt*' to a now familiar vista–another sea of slot machines–called '*The Carnival*'. We spot the next ride–'The House of Grandish'. The queue is posted as 30 minutes. It hardly moves. As we near the front, the reason becomes clear. This ride is shoebox sized. It takes 4 people at a time. Each session takes 4½ minutes. As we crawl to the front of the queue, Segaworld is suddenly revealed to me as a glitzy con-trick.

'*We anticipate that a true Segaworld experience will take four hours'*, so we arrived at 2.00 pm for a 6.00 pm departure. It is now 4.30, a *Segaperson* tells me that queues are over an hour downstairs, so we are going to miss out on three out of eight rides.

The floor manager is summoned. *Virtual tough-luck-mate. Shouldn't come at busy time.* As prickly as *Sonic the Hedgehog.*

I ask to see the *Segaboss*. Paul Smith, Operations Manager arrives. *Yes it's very busy, but we are nowhere near our fire certificate capacity. We are the victims of our own success. If you're got a complaint write in on Monday.*

Some victim, some success. It is us, the customer, who are the victims. While *Segaworld* counts the money, we stand in queues. Well I have got a complaint—three as it happens.

Complaint number 1 is that you are sold something that is not there. There is not the capacity in the riders to satisfy the visitor admissions. But you've paid your money up front. Its like paying in advance to get into a supermarket and finding the shelves empty. Every now and again there is a delivery of bread but you won't all get some.

Complaint number two is that the rides are a side-show–the main space is devoted to paying slot machines–acres of them. So in effect you pay £12 admission to a fancy amusement arcade.

And complaint number three is that the future has sadly not arrived. The rides are unimaginative, largely old tech. This is not how I understand interactive virtual reality. There is little total immersion (except is Space Mission, but even here the graphics are poor quality). You are not in control of anything. Interactivity is confined to mindlessly bashing a *fire* button. You do not make choices, you do not interact with other people, you follow a set path. It all lacks sophistication.

To be brutally frank, the games on my PC, the movie *Independence Day*, beat *Segaworld* hands down. Or as Louisa (age 12) put it, the best ride of the day was on the Bakerloo line train to get there.

Source: *The Times*, 14 December, 1996.

Questions

1. Analyse the opportunities and threats which led to the opening of segaworld.
2. What type of leisure activity is Segaworld and how did its opening of affect the competitive environment in this sector?
3. Account for the criticisms of Segaworld.
4. The author notes of Segaworld that 'sadly the future has not yet arrived'. What was meant by his statement and to what extent has virtual leisure replaced other forms of leisure?

Task 12.2: Fast Forward to the Future: Video on Demand

Dial a pizza? Half an hour later a spotty boy weaves down your street on an old Honda moped. Dial a video? Perhaps a similar scene springs to mind. A fleet of battered Hondas, panniers full of cassettes.

Not if BT have their way.

From today in BT's pilot area you can have VOD, or video-on-demand. To use the system you need a set-top decoder, a remote control device and of course a telephone line. Choose VOD from the remote control and a menu appears on the screen. You're now on-line to the VOD film database. You can browse through a comprehensive range of video titles, request a synopsis of the movie, a cast list or the running time.

Tap in few more commands and the video of your choice is downloaded to your decoder. You can choose to watch the film now or later on. The problem of the popular new release always out on rental on the night you want to take it out from the local video store is digitally solved. The trials being conducted at present also allow you to choose a range of TV shows including sports, children's programmes, soaps and comedy.

Steve Main, BT's Director of Visual and Broadcasting Services, explained that the company will charge between £1 and £3 per film to compete head-on with video rental stores, for whom a nationwide VOD system poses a serious threat.

But why BT's sudden interest in films? Competition from cable TV and mercury means that BT is forced to innovate to keep its market share in a fast-changing environment and it BT fails to capture the emerging VOD market, it will be lost to competitors. So whilst the cable operators are offering telephone services in competition with BT, BT is fighting back by offering entertainment *via* its telephone lines.

However, VOD technology doesn't stop at the movies. Its scope is enormous and could include home shopping, news services, specialist services, banking and reservation services.

In fact, holidays on demand are already possible in the BT pilot programme. Menus allow you to browse through various locations, seeing short video clips of the scenery, hotel facilities and local leisure pursuits. If you like what you see you can make an instant reservation, choosing your dates, your hotels and your airport of departure.

Source: The author, from new cuttings (1994).

Questions

1. What are the constituent parts of VOD technology?
2. What is the likely impact of VOD technology for the leisure and tourism sector?
3. This article was written is 1994. Evaluate the success of VOD since this pilot scheme.
4. What other specialized leisure or tourism services could use VOD technology?

Task 12.3: Cybersky's the Limit?

- ***1994:*** If you need to by a book you'll have to visit a bookshop or telephone one that does mail order.
- ***1995:*** Amazon.com started the Internet market in book sales.
- ***1997:*** Amazon becomes the third largest bookseller in the USA, as sales reach $148 million.
- ***1998:*** WH Smith (UK) acquires for £9.4 million bookshop.co.uk, Europe's largest on-line retail site, selling more than 1.4 million book titles and 50000 CDs, videos and computer games. This is seen by analysts as a defensive/offensive more against Amazon

as well as a way to capture a growing market. In 1997 Internet sales in the UK were worth about £200000, and are forecast to increase to £800000 by 2000.

Analysts say that the growth of on-line sales is not necessarily at the expense of high street booksellers—but rather that it is generating extra sales. The reasons for this are several. First, on-line bookstores offer substantial discounts which can be as high as 40 per cent. Second, interactive screens entice potential purchasers with lists of bestsellers, recommendations tailored to personal interests, reviews of books extracts, and interviews with the authors.

On-line selling costs are cheaper not only because of cheaper premises costs and lower staff costs but also because of minimal stock costs–Internet bookstores only take the stock when a customer has ordered a book. The publishing houses are already moving towards smaller print runs and this could lead eventually printing on demand which would further reduce costs of returns and holding stocks.

However, despite all these benefits Internet bookstores are still no making profits: In 1997, Amazon reported losses of $28.6 million. But, investors are clearly optimistic about the future since the price of Internet shares, including Amazon, have risen sharply.

Questions

1. What are the benefits of on-line sales to consumers and retailers?
2. What areas should be audited when conducting an opportunities and threats analysis?
3. Conduct an opportunities and threats analysis on a named booksellers that operates high street outlets.
4. Evaluate the impact of on-line sales elsewhere in the leisure and tourism sector.

